HOLISTIC HEALTH AND FITNESS
DRILLS AND EXERCISES

OCTOBER 2020

DISTRIBUTION RESTRICTION: Approved for public release; distribution is unlimited.

This publication supersedes chapters 7–10 and appendixes B, C, and E of FM 7-22, dated 26 October 2012.

HEADQUARTERS, DEPARTMENT OF THE ARMY

This publication is available at the Army Publishing Directorate site (https://armypubs.army.mil/) and the Central Army Registry site (https://atiam.train.army.mil/catalog/dashboard).

Printed by 4th Watch Publishing Co. For bulk Government-only orders go to: USGOVPUB.COM

Army Techniques Publication
No. 7-22.02

Headquarters
Department of the Army
Washington, D.C., 01 October 2020

HOLISTIC HEALTH AND FITNESS DRILLS AND EXERCISES

Contents

Page

PREFACE.. xv

INTRODUCTION xix

Chapter 1   PHYSICAL TRAINING DRILLS 1-1
Drill and Ceremony.. 1-1
Platoon Assembly.. 1-2
Platoon Reassembly.. 1-3
Preparation Drills 1-7
Activity Drills 1-8
Recovery Drills 1-9

Chapter 2   POSITIONS AND GRIPS 2-1
Positions... 2-1
Squat 2-1
Front Leaning Rest 2-2
Six-Point Stance 2-2
Straddle Stance 2-3
Forward Leaning Stance 2-3
Prone 2-3
Supine... 2-3
Half-Kneeling 2-4
Sitting.. 2-4

Grips 2-5
Closed... 2-5
Open 2-5
Underhand 2-5
Overhand 2-5
Neutral 2-5
Hook 2-6
Alternating Grip... 2-6

Chapter 3   PREPARATION DRILLS 3-1
The Preparation Drill 3-1
1. Bend and Reach 3-1
2. Rear Lunge 3-2

DISTRIBUTION RESTRICTION: Approved for public release; distribution is unlimited.

*This publication supersedes chapters 7–10 and appendixes B, C, and E of FM 7-22, dated 26 October 2012.

3. High Jumper 3-3
4. Rower 3-4
5. Squat Bender 3-5
6. Windmill 3-6
7. Forward Lunge 3-7
8. Prone Row 3-8
9. Bent-Leg Body Twist 3-8
10. Push-Up 3-8

Preparation Drill (Modified) (PD MOD) **3-10**
1. Bend and Reach (Modified) 3-10
2. Rear Lunge (Modified) 3-10
3. High Jumper (Modified) 3-12
4. Rower (Modified) 3-13
5. Squat Bender (Modified) 3-13
6. Windmill (Modified) 3-14
7. Forward Lunge (Modified) 3-16
8. Prone Row (Modified) 3-16
9. Bent-Leg Body Twist (Modified) 3-17
10. Push-Up (Modified) 3-18

Chapter 4   STABILITY DRILLS **4-1**

Hip Stability Drill (HSD) **4-1**
1. Lateral Leg Raise 4-1
2. Medial Leg Raise 4-2
3. Bent-Leg Lateral Raise 4-2
4. Single-Leg Tuck 4-3
5. Single Leg Over 4-4

Shoulder Stability Drill (SSD) **4-4**
1. I Raise 4-5
2. T Raise 4-6
3. Y Raise 4-6
4. L Raise 4-7
5. W Raise 4-8

Chapter 5   CONDITIONING DRILLS **5-1**

Conditioning Drill 1 (CD1) **5-1**
1. Power Jump 5-1
2. V-Up 5-2
3. Mountain Climber 5-3
4. Leg-Tuck and Twist 5-4
5. Single-Leg Push-Up 5-4

Conditioning Drill 1 (Modified) (CD1 MOD) **5-5**
1. Power Jump (Modified) 5-5
2. V-Up (Modified) 5-6
3. Mountain Climber (Modified) 5-7
4. Leg-Tuck and Twist (Modified) 5-8
5. Single-Leg Push-Up (Modified) 5-9

Conditioning Drill 2 (CD2) **5-9**
1. Turn and Lunge 5-9
2. Supine Bicycle 5-10
3. Half Jack 5-11
4. Swimmer 5-12
5. 8-Count T Push-Up 5-12

Conditioning Drill 3 (CD3) **5-13**

   1. Y Squat 5-13
   2. Single-Leg Deadlift 5-14
   3. Side-To-Side Knee Lifts 5-15
   4. Front Kick Alternate Toe Touch 5-16
   5. Tuck Jump 5-17
   6. Straddle Run Forward And Backward 5-18
   7. Half-Squat Laterals 5-19
   8. Frog Jumps Forward and Backward 5-20
   9. Alternate ¼-Turn Jump 5-21
   10. Alternate Staggered Squat Jump 5-22

Chapter 6   **CLIMBING AND GUERILLA DRILLS** **6-1**

   Climbing Drill 1 (CL1) **6-1**
   1. Straight-Arm Pull 6-1
   2. Heel Hook 6-2
   3. Pull-Up 6-3
   4. Leg Tuck 6-4
   5. Alternating Grip Pull-Up 6-5

   Climbing Drill 2 (CL2) **6-6**
   1. Flexed-Arm Hang 6-7
   2. Heel Hook 6-8
   3. Pull-Up 6-8
   4. Leg Tuck 6-8
   5. Alternating Grip Pull-Up 6-8

   Guerilla Drill (GD) **6-8**
   1. Shoulder Roll 6-8
   2. Lunge Walk 6-9
   3. Soldier Carry 6-9

Chapter 7   **RUNNING DRILLS** **7-1**

   Running Drill 1: Foot Strike (RUD1) **7-1**
   1. Heel Strike 7-1
   2. Heel Run In Place 7-2
   3. 8-Count Foot Strike 7-3
   4. Run In Place 1 7-4
   5. Run In Place 2 7-5

   Running Drill 2: Strength (RUD2) **7-6**
   1. Double-Leg Hop 7-6
   2. Single-Leg Hop 7-6
   3. Skip In Place 7-7
   4. Toes In and Out 7-8
   5. Criss Cross 7-8
   6. Pendulum 7-9
   7. Alternate Twist Jump 7-9
   8. Hip Raise Push-Up 7-10
   9. Single-Leg Hip Raise Push-Up 7-11
   10. Single-Leg Out Hip Raise Push-Up 7-11

   Running Drill 3: Runner's Position (RUD3) **7-12**
   1. Pose Weight Shift 7-12
   2. Pose Pull 7-13
   3. Alternate Pose Pull 7-14

   Running Drill 4: Fall (RUD4) **7-15**
   1. Timber Fall 7-15
   2. Timber Fall In Pose 7-16

3. Wall Fall 7-17
4. Wall Fall In Pose 7-18
5. Stretch Cord Fall 7-18
6. Partner Assisted Fall 7-19
7. Kneeling Timber Fall 7-20
8. Sprint Start 7-20

Running Drill 5: Pull (RUD5) **7-21**
1. Walk Progression 7-21
2. Pony 7-22
3. Pull Back 7-23
4. Elevated Pull Back 7-24
5. Kick Start 7-24

Running Drill 6: Combinations (RUD6) **7-26**
1. Change of Support 7-26
2. Hop in Place 7-27
3. Hop Forward 7-28
4. Run in Pose 7-29
5. Backwards Run 7-29

Running Drill 7: Corrections (RUD7) **7-30**
1. Hands in Front 7-30
2. Hands Behind 7-31
3. Hands on Back 7-31
4. Hands on Belly 7-32
5. Shin Burn 7-32
6. Infantry Run 7-33
7. Battle Buddy 7-34

Chapter 8   **MILITARY MOVEMENT DRILLS** **8-1**

Military Movement Drill 1 (MMD1) **8-1**
1. Vertical 8-1
2. Lateral 8-2
3. Shuttle Sprint 8-2

Military Movement Drill 2 (MMD2) **8-3**
1. Power Skip 8-3
2. Crossover 8-4
3. Crouch Run 8-5

Chapter 9   **MEDICINE BALL DRILLS** **9-1**

Medicine Ball Drill 1 (MB1) **9-1**
1. Chest Pass Lateral 9-1
2. Alternating Side-Arm Throw 9-2
3. Diagonal Chop 9-2
4. Slam 9-3
5. Underhand Wall Throw 9-4

Medicine Ball Drill 2 (MB2) **9-5**
1. Diagonal Chop Throw 9-5
2. Kneeling Side-Arm Throw 9-6
3. Sumo Wall Throw 9-7
4. Sit-Up Throw 9-8
5. Rainbow Slam 9-8

Chapter 10   **SUSPENSION TRAINING DRILLS** **10-1**

Suspension Training Drill 1 (ST1) **10-1**
1. Suspension Push-Up 10-1

2. Incline Calf Raise...10-2
3. Decline I-T-Y Raise 10-2
4. Assisted Squat..10-3
5. Decline Biceps Curl 10-3
Suspension Training Drill 2 (ST2)...**10-4**
1. Assisted Lateral Lunge 10-4
2. Suspension Leg-Tuck and Pike..10-5
3. Decline Pull-Up 10-6
4. Suspension Hamstring Curl..10-7
5. Assisted Single Leg Squat 10-7
6. Suspended Climbing Drills 1 and 2...10-9

Chapter 11   LANDMINE DRILLS...**11-1**
Landmine Drill 1 (LM1) **11-1**
1. Straight-Leg Deadlift..11-1
2. Diagonal Press 11-2
3. Rear Lunge 11-3
4.180-Degree Landmine...11-3
5. Lateral Lunge 11-4
Landmine Drill 2 (LM2) **11-6**
1. Diagonal Lift To Press 11-6
2. Single-Arm Chest Press...11-7
3. 180-Degree Landmine Kneeling..11-7
4. Bent-Over Row 11-8
5. Rear Lunge to Press...11-9

Chapter 12   PREGNANCY AND POSTPARTUM PHYSICAL TRAINING DRILLS..................**12-1**
Pregnancy and Postpartum Physical Training 12-1
1. Reverse Sit-Up 12-1
2. Oblique Sit-Up 12-2
3. Modified Sit-Up 12-3
4. Standing Trunk Curve...12-4
5. Deep Sumo Squat 12-4
6. Pelvic Clock 12-6

Chapter 13   STRENGTH TRAINING CIRCUIT..**13-1**
Strength Training 13-1
1. Sumo Squat 13-1
2. Straight-Leg Deadlift..13-2
3. Forward Lunge 13-3
4. 8-Count Step-Up..13-4
5a. Pull-Up 13-6
5b: Straight-Arm Pull 13-6
6. Supine Chest Press 13-7
7. Bent-Over Row 13-8
8. Overhead Push-Press 13-8
9. Supine Body Twist 13-9
10. Leg Tuck 13-10

Chapter 14   FREE WEIGHT TRAINING..**14-1**
Free Weights 14-1
Free Weight Core Training Exercises 14-1
Free Weight Assistive Training Exercises 14-9

Chapter 15   STRENGTH TRAINING MACHINE DRILL..**15-1**
Strength Training Machines 15-1
Leg Press..15-1

Leg Curl 15-3
Lateral Raise 15-4
Single-Arm Lateral Raise 15-5
Overhead Press 15-6
Lat Pull-Down 15-7
Seated Row 15-9
Trunk Extension 15-11
Modified Trunk Extension 15-12
Triceps Extension 15-12
Chest Press 15-13
Trunk Flexion 15-15
Modified Trunk Flexion 15-16

Chapter 16   RECOVERY DRILLS 16-1

The Recovery Drill 16-1
1. Overhead Arm Pull 16-1
2. Rear Lunge 16-2
3. Extend and Flex 16-3
4. Thigh Stretch 16-3
5. Single-Leg Over 16-4
6. Groin Stretch 16-4
7. Calf Stretch 16-5
8. Hamstring Stretch 16-6

The Recovery Drill (Modified) 16-6
1. Overhead Arm Pull (Modified) 16-6
2. Rear Lunge (Modified) 16-7
3. Extend and Flex (Modified) 16-8
4. Thigh Stretch (Modified) 16-10
5. Single-Leg Over (Modified) 16-10
6. Groin Stretch (Modified) 16-11
7. Calf Stretch (Modified) 16-12
8. Hamstring Stretch (Modified) 16-13

Chapter 17   PREVENTIVE MAINTENANCE CHECKS AND SERVICES DRILLS 17-1
Preventive Maintenance Checks and Services 17-1
1. Spine 17-1
2. Ankle 17-6
3. Knee 17-7
4. Hip 17-8
5. Shoulder 17-9
6. Arm 17-10

SOURCE NOTES .... Source Notes-1

GLOSSARY Glossary-1

REFERENCES References-1

INDEX Index-1

Figures

Figure 1-1. Platoon rectangular formation 1-3
Figure 1-2. Platoon rectangular formation extended and uncovered 1-3
Figure 1-3. Forming a company, company in line with platoons in column 1-4

Figure 1-4. Company extended and uncovered, company in line with platoons in column 1-4

Figure 1-5. Formation of company en masse 1-5

Figure 1-6. Company en masse extended and uncovered 1-5

Figure 1-7. Platoon formation en masse 1-6

Figure 1-8. Platoon formation extended and covered 1-6

Figure 2-1. Positions 2-1

Figure 2-2. Squat position 2-2

Figure 2-3. Front Leaning Rest position 2-2

Figure 2-4. Six-Point Stance position 2-2

Figure 2-5. Straddle Stance position 2-3

Figure 2-6. The Forward Leaning Stance position 2-3

Figure 2-7. Prone position 2-4

Figure 2-8. Supine position 2-4

Figure 2-9. Half-Kneeling position 2-4

Figure 2-10. Sitting position 2-4

Figure 2-11. Grips 2-5

Figure 3-1. PD1 Bend and Reach 3-1

Figure 3-2. PD2 Rear Lunge 3-2

Figure 3-3. PD2 Proper technique to execute the Rear Lunge 3-2

Figure 3-4. PD3 High Jumper 3-3

Figure 3-5. PD4 Rower 3-4

Figure 3-6. PD4 Proper technique to execute the Rower 3-4

Figure 3-7. PD5 Squat Bender 3-5

Figure 3-8. PD6 Windmill 3-6

Figure 3-9. PD6 Proper technique to execute the Windmill 3-6

Figure 3-10. PD7 Forward Lunge 3-7

Figure 3-11. PD8 Prone Row 3-8

Figure 3-12. PD9 Bent-Leg Body Twist 3-9

Figure 3-13. PD10 Push-Up 3-9

Figure 3-14. PD MOD1 Bend and Reach (modified) 3-11

Figure 3-15. PD MOD2 Rear Lunge (modified) 3-11

Figure 3-16. PD MOD3 High Jumper (modified) 3-12

Figure 3-17. PD MOD4 Rower (modified) 3-13

Figure 3-18. PD MOD5 Squat Bender (modified) 3-14

Figure 3-19. PD MOD6 Windmill (modified) 3-15

Figure 3-20. PD MOD6 Windmill (modified) alternative movement 3-15

Figure 3-21. PD MOD7 Forward Lunge (modified) 3-16

Figure 3-22. PD MOD8 Prone Row (modified) 3-17

Figure 3-23. PD MOD8 Prone Row (modified) alternative movement 3-17

Figure 3-24. PD MOD9 Bent-Leg Body Twist (modified) 3-18

Figure 3-25. PD MOD10 Push-Up (modified) 3-18

Figure 4-1. HSD1 Lateral Leg Raise 4-1

Figure 4-2. HSD2 Medial Leg Raise 4-2

Figure 4-3. HSD3 Bent-Leg Lateral Raise 4-3

Figure 4-4. HSD4 Single-Leg Tuck 4-4

Figure 4-5. HSD5 Single Leg Over 4-5

Figure 4-6. SSD1 I Raise 4-5

Figure 4-7. SSD2 T raise 4-6

Figure 4-8. SSD3 Y Raise 4-7

Figure 4-9. SSD4 L Raise 4-7

Figure 4-10. SSD5 W Raise with improper form 4-8

Figure 4-11. SSD5 W Raise 4-8

Figure 5-1. CD1.1 Power Jump 5-2

Figure 5-2. CD1.2 V-Up 5-3

Figure 5-3. CD1.3 Mountain Climber 5-3

Figure 5-4. CD1.4 Leg-Tuck and Twist 5-4

Figure 5-5. CD1.5 Single-Leg Push-up 5-5

Figure 5-6. CD1 MOD1 Power Jump (modified) 5-6

Figure 5-7. CD1 MOD2 V-Up (modified) 5-6

Figure 5-8. CD1 MOD3 Mountain Climber (modified) 5-7

Figure 5-9. CD1 MOD4 Leg-Tuck and Twist (modified) 5-8

Figure 5-10. CD1 MOD5 Push-Up (modified) 5-9

Figure 5-11. CD2.1 Turn and Lunge 5-10

Figure 5-12. CD2.2 Supine Bicycle 5-11

Figure 5-13. CD2.3 Half Jack 5-11

Figure 5-14. CD2.4 Swimmer 5-12

Figure 5-15. CD2.5 8-Count T-Push-Up 5-13

Figure 5-16. CD3.1 Y Squat 5-14

Figure 5-17. CD3.2 Single-Leg Deadlift 5-15

Figure 5-18. CD3.3 Side-to-Side Knee Lifts 5-16

Figure 5-19. CD3.4 Front Kick Alternate Toe Touch 5-17

Figure 5-20. CD3.5 Tuck Jump 5-18

Figure 5-21. CD3.6 Straddle Run Forward and Backward 5-19

Figure 5-22. CD3.7 Half-Squat Laterals 5-20

Figure 5-23. CD3.8 Frog Jumps Forward and Backward 5-21

Figure 5-24. CD3.9 Alternate ¼-Turn Jump 5-22

Figure 5-25. CD3.10 Alternate Staggered Squat Jump 5-23

Figure 6-1. CL1.1 Straight Arm Pull 6-2

Figure 6-2. CL1.2 Heel Hook 6-3

Figure 6-3. CL1.3 Pull-Up 6-4

Figure 6-4. CL1.4 Leg Tuck 6-5

Figure 6-5. CL1.5 Alternating Grip Pull-Up 6-6

Figure 6-6. CL2.1 Flexed-Arm Hang 6-7

Figure 6-7. GD1 Shoulder Roll 6-8

Figure 6-8. GD2 Lunge Walk 6-9

Figure 6-9. GD3 Soldier Carry 6-10

Figure 7-1. RUD1.1 Heel Strike 7-2

Figure 7-2. RUD1.2 Heel Run in Place 7-3

Figure 7-3. RUD1.3 8-Count Foot Strike 7-4

Figure 7-4. RUD1.4 Run in Place 1 7-5

Figure 7-5. RUD1.5 Run in Place 2 7-5

Figure 7-6. RUD2.1 Double-Leg Hop 7-6

Figure 7-7. RUD2.2 Single-Leg Hop 7-7

Figure 7-8. RUD2.3 Skip in Place 7-7

Figure 7-9. RUD2.4 Toes In and Out 7-8

Figure 7-10. RUD2.5 Criss Cross..7-8

Figure 7-11. RUD2.6 Pendulum 7-9

Figure 7-12. RUD2.7 Alternate Twist Jump 7-10

Figure 7-13. RUD2.8 Hip Raise Push-Up 7-11

Figure 7-14. RUD2.9 Single-Leg Hip Raise Push-Up 7-11

Figure 7-15. RUD2.10 Single-Leg Out Hip Raise Push-Up 7-12

Figure 7-16. RUD3.1 Pose Weight Shift 7-13

Figure 7-17. RUD3.2 Pose Pull 7-14

Figure 7-18. RUD3.3 Alternate Pose Pull 7-15

Figure 7-19. RUD4.1 Timber Fall 7-16

Figure 7-20. RUD4.2 Timber Fall in Pose 7-16

Figure 7-21. RUD4.3 Wall Fall 7-17

Figure 7-22. RUD4.4 Wall Fall in Pose 7-18

Figure 7-23. RUD4.5 Stretch Cord Fall 7-19

Figure 7-24. RUD4.6 Partner Assisted Fall 7-19

Figure 7-25. RUD4.7 Kneeling Timber Fall 7-20

Figure 7-26. RUD4.8 Sprint Start 7-21

Figure 7-27. RUD5.1 Walk Progression 7-21

Figure 7-28. RUD5.2 Pony 7-22

Figure 7-29. RUD5.3 Pull Back 7-23

Figure 7-30. RUD5.4 Elevated Pull Back 7-24

Figure 7-31. RUD5.5 Kick Start 7-25

Figure 7-34. RUD6.1 Change of Support 7-26

Figure 7-35. RUD6.2 Hop in Place 7-27

Figure 7-36. RUD6.3 Hop Forward 7-28

Figure 7-37. RUD6.4 Run in Pose...7-29

Figure 7-38. RUD6.5 Backwards Run 7-30

Figure 7-39. RUD7.1 Hands in Front...7-30

Figure 7-40. RUD7.2 Hands Behind 7-31

Figure 7-41. RUD7.3 Hands on Back 7-31

Figure 7-42. RUD7.4 Hands on Belly 7-32

Figure 7-43. RUD7.5 Shin Burn 7-33

Figure 7-44. RUD7.6 Infantry Run 7-33

Figure 7-45. RUD7.7 Battle Buddy 7-34

Figure 8-1. MMD1.1 Vertical 8-1

Figure 8-2. MMD1.2 Lateral 8-2

Figure 8-3. MMD1.3 Shuttle Sprint 8-3

Figure 8-4. MMD2.1 Power Skip 8-4

Figure 8-5. MMD2.2 Crossover 8-5

Figure 8-6. MMD2.3 Crouch Run 8-6

Figure 9-1. MB1.1 Chest Pass Lateral 9-1

Figure 9-2. MB1.2 Alternating Side-Arm Throw 9-2

Figure 9-3. MB1.3 Diagonal Chop 9-3

Figure 9-4. MB1.4 Slam 9-4

Figure 9-5. MB1.5 Underhand Wall Throw 9-5

Figure 9-6. MB2.1 Diagonal Chop Throw 9-6

Figure 9-7. MB2.2 Kneeling Side-Arm Throw 9-7

Figure 9-8. MB2.3 Sumo Wall Throw 9-7

Figure 9-9. MB2.4 Sit-Up Throw 9-8

Figure 9-10. MB2.5 Rainbow Slam 9-9

Figure 10-1. ST1.1 Suspension Push-Up 10-1

Figure 10-2. ST1.2 Incline Calf Raise 10-2

Figure 10-3. ST1.3 Decline I-T-Y Raise 10-3

Figure 10-4. ST1.4 Assisted Squat 10-3

Figure 10-5. ST1.5 Decline Biceps Curl 10-4

Figure 10-6. ST2.1 Assisted Lateral Lunge 10-5

Figure 10-7. ST2.2 Suspension Leg-Tuck and Pike 10-5

Figure 10-8. ST2.3 Decline Pull-Up 10-6

Figure 10-9. ST2.4 Suspension Hamstring Curl 10-7

Figure 10-10. ST2.5 Assisted Single-Leg Squat 10-8

Figure 10-11. ST2.5a Assisted Single-Leg Squat with alternative movement 10-8

Figure 10-12. ST2.6 Suspended Straight-Arm Pull 10-9

Figure 10-13. ST2.6 Suspended Heel Hook 10-9

Figure 10-14. ST2.6. Suspended Leg Tuck 10-9

Figure 10-15. ST2.6 Suspended Pull-Up 10-9

Figure 10-16. ST2.6 Suspended Alternating Grip Pull-Up 10-10

Figure 10-17. ST2.6 Suspended Flexed Arm Hang 10-10

Figure 11-1. LM1.1 Straight-Leg Deadlift 11-2

Figure 11-2. LM1.2 Diagonal Press 11-3

Figure 11-3. LM1.3 Rear Lunge 11-3

Figure 11-4. LM1.4 180-Degree Landmine 11-4

Figure 11-5. LM1.5 Lateral Lunge 11-5

Figure 11-6. LM2.1 Diagonal Lift to Press 11-6

Figure 11-7. LM2.2 Single-Arm Chest Press 11-7

Figure 11-8. LM2.3 180-Degree Landmine Kneeling 11-8

Figure 11-9. LM2.4 Bent-Over Row 11-9

Figure 11-10. LM2.5 Rear Lunge to Press 11-9

Figure 12-1. P3T1 Reverse Sit-Up 12-2

Figure 12-2. P3T2 Oblique Sit-Up 12-3

Figure 12-3. P3T3 Modified Sit-Up 12-3

Figure 12-4. P3T3 Modified Sit-Up—head lift 12-3

Figure 12-5. P3T4 Standing Trunk Curve 12-4

Figure 12-6. P3T4 Seated Trunk Curve 12-4

Figure 12-7. P3T5 Deep Sumo Squat 12-5

Figure 12-8. P3T5 Deep Sumo Squat—weight-assisted 12-5

Figure 12-9. P3T5 Deep Sumo Squat—from Standing position without weight 12-5

Figure 12-10. P3T6 Pelvic Clock 12-6

Figure 13-1. STC1 Sumo Squat 13-2

Figure 13-2. STC2 Straight-Leg Deadlift 13-3

Figure 13-3. STC3 Forward Lunge 13-4

Figure 13-4. STC4 8-Count Step-up 13-5

Figure 13-5. STC5A Pull-up 13-6

Figure 13-6. STC5B Straight-Arm Pull 13-7

Figure 13-7. STC6 Supine Chest Press 13-7

Figure 13-8. STC7 Bent-Over Row 13-8

Figure 13-9. STC8 Overhead Push-Press 13-9

Figure 13-10. STC9 Supine Body Twist 13-9

Figure 13-11. STC10 Leg Tuck 13-10

Figure 14-1. FW1 Front Squat 14-2

Figure 14-2. FW2 Back Squat 14-3

Figure 14-3. FW3 Deadlift—straight bar 14-4

Figure 14-4. FW3 Deadlift—kettlebells 14-4

Figure 14-5. FW3 Straight-Leg Deadlift 14-5

Figure 14-6. FW4 Bench Press—straight bar 14-6

Figure 14-7. FW4 Bench Press—dumbbell 14-7

Figure 14-8. FW4 Bench Press—kettlebell 14-7

Figure 14-9. FW4 Bench Press—decline 14-8

Figure 14-10. FW5 Incline Bench 14-8

Figure 14-11. FW6 Sumo Deadlift 14-10

Figure 14-12. FW7 Heel Raise 14-11

Figure 14-13. FW8 Bent-Over Row 14-12

Figure 14-14. FW9 Single-Arm Bent-Over Row 14-13

Figure 14-15. FW10 Upright Row—straight bar 14-14

Figure 14-16. FW10 Upright Row—kettlebell 14-14

Figure 14-17. FW11 Overhead Push-Press 14-15

Figure 14-18. FW12 Bent-Arm Lateral Raise 14-16

Figure 14-19. FW13 Shrug 14-17

Figure 14-20. FW14 Pull Over—single dumbbell 14-18

Figure 14-21. FW14 Pull Over—double dumbbells 14-18

Figure 14-22. FW15 Overhead Triceps Extension 14-19

Figure 14-23. FW16 Biceps Curl 14-20

Figure 14-24. FW17 Weighted Trunk Flexion 14-20

Figure 14-25. FW18 Weighted Trunk Extension 14-21

Figure 15-1. STM Leg Press 15-2

Figure 15-2. STM Single-Leg Press 15-2

Figure 15-3. STM Leg Curl 15-3

Figure 15-4. STM Single-Leg Curl 15-4

Figure 15-5. STM Lateral Raise 15-5

Figure 15-6. STM Single-Arm Lateral Raise 15-5

Figure 15-7. STM Overhead Press 15-6

Figure 15-8. STM Single-Arm Overhead Press 15-7

Figure 15-9. STM Lat Pull-Down 15-8

Figure 15-10. STM Single-Arm Lat Pull-Down 15-9

Figure 15-11. STM Seated Row 15-10

Figure 15-12. STM Single-Arm Seated Row 15-11

Figure 15-13. STM Trunk Extension 15-12

Figure 15-14. STM Triceps Extension 15-12

Figure 15-15. STM Single-Arm Triceps Extension 15-13

Figure 15-16. STM Chest Press 15-14

Figure 15-17. STM Single-Arm Chest Press 15-15

Figure 15-18. STM Trunk Flexion 15-16

Figure 16-1. RD1 Overhead Arm Pull 16-1

Figure 16-2. RD2 Rear Lunge 16-2

Figure 16-3. RD3 Extend and Flex 16-3

Figure 16-4. RD4 Thigh Stretch 16-3

Figure 16-5. RD5 Single-Leg Over 16-4

Figure 16-6. RD6 Groin Stretch 16-5

Figure 16-7. RD7 Calf Stretch 16-5

Figure 16-8. RD8 Hamstring Stretch 16-6

Figure 16-9. RD MOD1 Overhead Arm Pull (modified) 16-7

Figure 16-10. RD MOD2 Rear Lunge (modified) 16-8

ATP 7-22.02

Figure 16-11. RD MOD3 Extend and Flex (modified) 16-9

Figure 16-12. RD MOD3 Extend and Flex (modified)—standing 16-9

Figure 16-13. RD MOD4 Thigh Stretch (modified) 16-10

Figure 16-14. RD MOD5 Single-Leg Over (modified) 16-11

Figure 16-15. RD MOD6 Groin Stretch (modified) 16-12

Figure 16-16. RD MOD7 Calf Stretch (modified) 16-12

Figure 16-17. RD MOD8 Hamstring (modified) 16-13

Figure 16-18. RD MOD8 Hamstring (modified)—single leg 16-13

Figure 17-1. PMCS1 Spine—neck 17-2

Figure 17-2. PMCS1 Spine—mid-back seated 17-3

Figure 17-3. PMCS1 Spine—mid-back standing mobility 17-4

Figure 17-4. PMCS1 Spine—mid-back prone mobility 17-4

Figure 17-5. PMCS1 Spine—low back prone 17-5

Figure 17-6. PMCS1 Spine—low back standing 17-5

Figure 17-7. PMCS2 Ankle 17-6

Figure 17-8. PMCS2 Ankle—kneeling 17-6

Figure 17-9. PMCS3 Knee 17-7

Figure 17-10. PMCS4 Hip 17-8

Figure 17-11. PMCS4 Hip—supine 17-8

Figure 17-12. PMCS5 Shoulder—partner assisted 17-9

Figure 17-13. PMCS5 Shoulder 17-9

Figure 17-14. PMCS6 Arm 17-10

Figure 17-15. PMCS6 Elbow and wrist 17-11

Tables

Table 1-1. Three examples of a modified Preparation Drill 1-7

Table 1-2. Physical training activities 1-8

This page intentionally left blank.

Preface

ATP 7-22.02, *Holistic Health and Fitness Drills and Exercises* includes drills and exercises for individual and organizational physical training programs. It is a companion to the physical readiness domain described in FM 7-22, *Holistic Health and Fitness*. The purpose of this publication is to provide exercise standards for Soldiers and leaders who need them in order to develop physical training programs. In situations where holistic health and fitness (H2F) resources are not available, Soldiers and units can use this content to standardize training.

The drills and exercises in this publication are designed to support building physical readiness and meet physical fitness standards. Testing standards are described in ATP 7-22.01 *Holistic Health and Fitness Testing* which describes the administration and evaluation procedures for the Occupational Physical Assessment Test (OPAT), Army Combat Fitness Test (ACFT), and Combat Water Survival Test (CWST).

The principal audience for doctrine is leaders at all organizational levels. Leaders include officers, warrant officers, noncommissioned officers, and those Army civilians in leadership positions. Trainers and educators throughout the Army will also use this publication.

Commanders, staffs, and subordinates at all levels ensure that H2F training programs are properly resourced and administered in accordance with requirements outlined in this ATP. Commanders, staffs, and subordinates ensure that their decisions and actions comply with applicable United States, international, and in some cases host-nation laws and regulations. Commanders at all levels ensure that their Soldiers operate in accordance with the law of war and the rules of engagement. (See FM 6-27/MCTP 11-10C.)

Demonstration videos of H2F test events and exercises are located on the Army Combat Fitness Test website at https://www.army.mil/acft/ and on the Central Army Registry website at https://atiam.train.army.mil/catalog/search?current=true&filetype=mp4&respect_date=5%2F1%2F2020&search_terms=CIMT. (Copy and paste this address after accessing the Central Army Registry website if the demonstrations do not populate.)

Terms included in the glossary are not codified Army terms. They are included only for clarity for the reader. This publication is not a proponent for any Army doctrine terms.

For emphasis, the names of specific drills and exercises are title cased in this publication only.

This doctrine and the regulations that support it apply to the Active Army, the Army National Guard/Army National Guard of the United States and the United States Army Reserve, unless otherwise stated.

The proponent for this publication is the United States Army Center for Initial Military Training (USACIMT), Training and Doctrine Command (TRADOC). Submit comments and recommendations for improvement of this field manual on DA Form 2028 (*Recommended Changes to Publications and Blank Forms*). To contact USACIMT:

Commander, Center for Initial Military Training
ATTN: Director Research and Analysis
210 Dillon Circle
Fort Eustis, VA 23604

This page intentionally left blank.

Acknowledgements

The copyright owners listed here have granted permission to reproduce material from their works. The Source Notes lists other sources of quotations and photographs.

Photos developed by the U.S. Army Center for Initial Military Training and produced at the Enterprise Media Center in Fort Eustis, Virginia.

Running drills discussed in chapter 7 courtesy Dr. Nicholas Romanov and Severin Romanov, Pose Method, Inc. Copyright © 2020 Pose Method Publishing, Inc.

This page intentionally left blank.

Introduction

Physical readiness is a cornerstone of Soldier readiness, and by extension, Army readiness. As such, drills and exercises are intrinsically linked to the physical readiness domain of the H2F system. The physical drills and exercises in H2F system are standardized so that no matter where they train, Soldiers can quickly understand the exercises and perform them safely. Unit-level physical training is typically conducted in a unit formation. All physical activity begins with preparation, stability, movement and running drills. All physical activity concludes with recovery drills.

Chapter 1, "Physical Training Drills," discusses the proper organization of Soldiers to conduct collective training sessions. This chapter includes drill and ceremony, command delivery, formations and an overview of the three types of drills: preparation drills, activity drills, and recovery drills.

Chapter 2, "Positions and Grips," covers the proper positions to execute various drills and exercises, as well as the proper techniques Soldiers should use during weight training.

Chapter 3, "Preparation Drills," contains the Preparation Drill (PD) and Preparation Drill (Modified) (PD MOD) that are conducted prior to executing any physical training session or H2F test event.

Chapter 4, "Stability Drills," includes the exercises Hip Stability Drill (HSD), Shoulder Stability Drill (SSD), and Four for the Core (4C).

Chapter 5, "Conditioning Drills," consists of four condition drills: Conditioning Drill 1 (CD1), Conditioning Drill 1 (Modified) (CD1 [MOD]), Conditioning Drill 2 (CD2), and Conditioning Drill 3 (CD3).

Chapter 6, "Climbing and Guerilla Drills," includes Climbing Drill 1 (CL1), Climbing Drill 2 (CL2), and Guerilla Drill (GD).

Chapter 7, "Running Drills," consists of the seven Running Drills (RD1–RD7).

Chapter 8, "Military Movement Drills," includes the exercises for Military Movement Drill 1 (MMD1) and Military Movement Drill 2 (MMD2).

Chapter 9, "Medicine Ball Drills," includes the exercises for Medicine Ball Drill 1 (MB1) and Medicine Ball Drill 2 (MB2).

Chapter 10, "Suspension Training Drills," consists of the exercises that make up Suspension Training Drill 1 (ST1) and Suspension Training Drill 2 (ST2).

Chapter 11, "Landmine Drills," includes exercises utilizing a free-weight training device known as a landmine and includes two drills: Landmine Drill 1 (LM1) and Landmine Drill 2 (LM2).

Chapter 12, "Pregnancy and Postpartum Physical Training Drills," includes specific exercises designed to assist female Soldiers during pregnancy and in recovery following childbirth.

Chapter 13, "Strength Training Circuit," consists of 10 exercise stations that use strength training equipment and climbing drill exercises.

Chapter 14, "Free Weight Training," includes 18 exercises using various free weight equipment.

Chapter 15, "Strength Training Machine Drill," includes instructions for ten machines and modified ways to use them.

Chapter 16, "Recovery Drills," includes the exercises Recovery Drill and Recovery Drill (Modified) (RD MOD) that are conducted at the conclusion of physical training sessions and H2F testing events.

Chapter 17, "Preventive Maintenance Checks and Services Drill," includes a series of six exercises that Soldiers can perform before conducting physical readiness training or include with exercises performed in the Recovery Drill.

EQUIPMENT SAFETY INSPECTIONS

Prior to executing any physical training program involving exercise equipment, users should be visibly inspect equipment and any components for serviceability. Equipment safety inspections should include, but are not limited to: stress cracks at welded seams on weight lifting bars; torn fabric or stitching on nylon sleds and pull straps; loose connections on pull-up bars; and cables, pedals, or other moveable accessories on strength training machines, rowing machines, and stationary bicycles. Defects may compromise the load bearing capability of equipment and present a potential safety hazard to the user.

Chapter 1

Physical Training Drills

DRILL AND CEREMONY

1-1. Physical training drills are a fundamental component of Army training. Drill and ceremony is one of the very first experiences for Soldiers upon entering initial military training. Every aspect of organized physical readiness training also incorporates physical training drills. Key components of any drill are command delivery, formation, assembly, and reassembly.

1-2. Paragraphs 1-8 through 1-10 discuss the importance of proper organization of Soldiers in collective training sessions. Having the right number of Soldiers organized into the right number of ranks improves the training effect. This cannot be underestimated. Invariably, performance reflects the quality of its commands. Indifferent commands produce indifferent performance. When a leader gives a verbal command distinctly, concisely, with energy, and with proper regard to rhythm, Soldier performance reflects it. See TC 3-21.5 for detailed information of command voice, posture, and presence.

1-3. The Army uses commands and cadence to instill confidence, demonstrate professionalism, and facilitate training. When Soldiers train individually, they should remember that the cadences and recovery between exercises have been designed to improve the training effect. Retaining those during individual training is strongly encouraged. It is a mark of discipline and professionalism. When Soldiers train in groups smaller than a platoon, variance from instructions in this section should not compromise the ability of the leader to see the Soldiers and the Soldiers to hear their leader.

COMMAND TYPES

1-4. The two types of commands used in physical training are preparatory commands and commands of execution. The preparatory command describes and specifies what is required. Leaders give all preparatory commands with rising voice inflection. The command of execution calls into action what has been prescribed. The interval between the two commands provides enough time to permit the Soldier to understand the first command before listening to the second one.

COMMAND DELIVERY

1-5. The physical training leader addresses Soldiers in formation for collective exercises. The leader commands movement or announces the name of an exercise from the Position of Attention. Exceptions are exercises that change position without returning to the Position of Attention.

> *Note.* Soldiers and leaders speak or yell the words in all capital letters. When leaders give commands, they emphasize and forcibly project the italicized words.

1-6. When Soldiers perform exercises, they assume the proper starting position of each exercise on the command, "STARTING POSITION, *MOVE*." When conducting exercises, a leader commands Soldiers to return to the Position of Attention from the terminating position of the exercise before he or she commands Soldiers to assume the starting position for the next exercise. Physical training leaders use the command, "POSITION OF ATTENTION, *MOVE*," to bring Soldiers to the Position of Attention from an exercise terminating position.

1-7. For example, the physical training leader would conduct exercise 4, Thigh Stretch in the Recovery Drill (known as RD) using the following:

- From the Position of Attention, the physical training leader commands, "THE THIGH STRETCH."
- Soldiers respond, "THE THIGH STRETCH."
- From the Position of Attention, the physical training leader commands, "STARTING POSITION, *MOVE*."
- The physical training leader and Soldiers assume the starting position for the Thigh Stretch.
- From the starting position, the physical training leader commands, "READY, STRETCH."
- To change position, the physical training leader first commands, "STARTING POSITION, *MOVE*."
- From the starting position, the physical training leader commands, "CHANGE POSITION, READY, STRETCH."
- Upon termination of the exercise, the physical training leader returns to the starting position before giving the command, "STARTING POSITION, *MOVE*."
- The physical training leader assumes the Position of Attention and commands, "POSITION OF ATTENTION, *MOVE*."

EXTENDED RECTANGULAR FORMATION

1-8.   The Army's traditional formation for physical training activities is the extended rectangular formation. It is best for platoon- to company-size formations because it is simple and easy to assume.

PLATOON ASSEMBLY

1-9.   The physical training leader positions a platoon-size unit in a line formation so that the unit is centered and five paces away from the physical training platform or leader after the unit has assumed the rectangular formation. Refer to figure 1-1. The physical training leader gives the following commands:

- "EXTEND TO THE LEFT, *MARCH*." Soldiers in the right flank file stand fast with their left arms extended sideward with palms down, fingers and thumbs extended and joined. All other Soldiers turn to the left and double-time forward. After taking the sufficient number of steps, all Soldiers face the front and extend both arms sideward with palms down, fingers and thumbs extended and joined. The distance between fingertips is about 12 inches and dress is to the right.
- "ARMS DOWNWARD, *MOVE*." The Soldiers lower their arms smartly to their sides. Soldiers in the right flank file lower their left arms to their sides.
- "LEFT, *FACE*." Soldiers execute the left face.
- "EXTEND TO THE LEFT, *MARCH*." Soldiers in the right flank file stand fast with their left arms extended sideward with palms down, fingers and thumbs extended and joined. All other Soldiers turn to the left and double-time forward. After taking the sufficient number of steps, all Soldiers face the front and extend both arms sideward with palms down, fingers and thumbs extended and joined. The distance between fingertips is about 12 inches and dress is to the right.
- "ARMS DOWNWARD, *MOVE*." Soldiers lower their arms smartly to their sides. Soldiers in the right flank file lower their left arms to their sides.
- "RIGHT, *FACE*." Soldiers execute the right face.
- "FROM FRONT TO REAR, *COUNT OFF*." The front Soldier in each column turns his or her head to the right rear, and then calls off, "ONE," and faces the front. Successive Soldiers in each column call off in turn "TWO," "THREE," "FOUR," and so on. The last Soldier in each column will not turn his or her head and eyes to the right while sounding off.
- "EVEN NUMBER TO THE LEFT, *UNCOVER*." Even-numbered Soldiers side step to the left squarely in the center of the interval, bringing their feet together. (See Figure 1-2.)

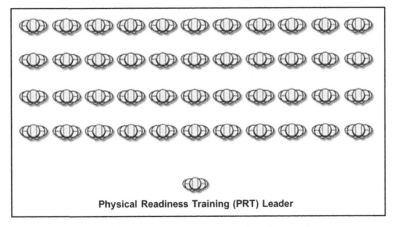

Figure 1-1. Platoon rectangular formation

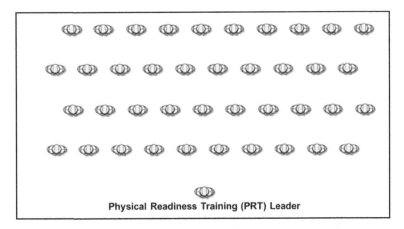

Figure 1-2. Platoon rectangular formation extended and uncovered

PLATOON REASSEMBLY

1-10. To reassemble the formation, the physical training leader commands, "ASSEMBLE TO THE RIGHT, *MARCH*." All Soldiers double-time to their original positions in the formation (see figure 1-1).

COMPANY IN LINE WITH PLATOONS IN COLUMN

1-11. The physical training leader positions a company-size unit in the extended rectangular formation from a company in line with platoons in column. He or she then adjusts the base platoon so that the company will be centered and five paces away from the physical training platform or leader after the company has assumed the rectangular formation. Refer to figure 1-3 on page 1-4. The physical training leader gives the commands specified in paragraph 1-15 to extend the formation (see figure 1-4 on page 1-4).

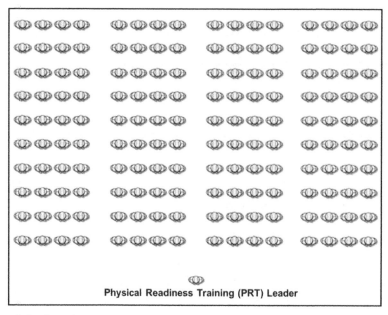

Figure 1-3. Forming a company, company in line with platoons in column

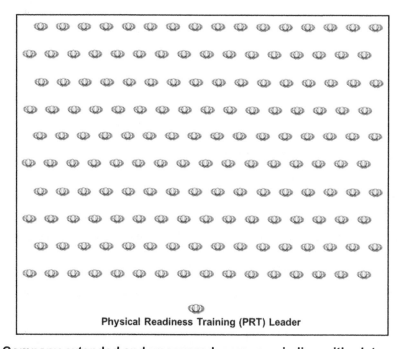

Figure 1-4. Company extended and uncovered, company in line with platoons in column

1-12. To reassemble the formation, the physical training leader commands, "ASSEMBLE TO THE RIGHT, *MARCH*." All Soldiers double-time to their original positions in the formation (see figure 1-3).

COMPANY FORMATION EN MASSE

1-13. The physical training leader positions a company-size unit in a rectangular formation. He or she first adjusts the base platoon so that the company will be centered and five paces away from the physical training platform or leader after the company has assumed the rectangular formation. Refer to figure 1-5. The physical training leader gives the commands specified in paragraph 1-10 to extend the formation (see figure 1-6).

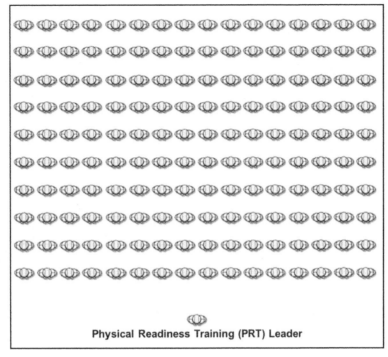

Figure 1-5. Formation of company en masse

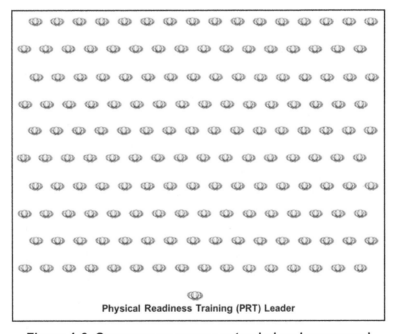

Figure 1-6. Company en masse extended and uncovered

1-14. To reassemble the formation, the physical training leader commands, "ASSEMBLE TO THE RIGHT, *MARCH*." All Soldiers double-time to their original positions in the formation (see figure 1-5).

PLATOON EXTENDED RECTANGULAR FORMATION, COVERED

1-15. The formation for Military Movement Drill (known as MMD) and Guerrilla Drill (known as GD) is a platoon extended rectangular formation, covered. The physical training leader positions the platoon in a line formation so the unit will be centered and five paces away from the physical training platform or leader after it assumes the extended rectangular formation (see figure 1-7). The physical training leader gives the following commands to extend the platoon formation covered (see figure 1-8):

- "EXTEND TO THE LEFT, *MARCH*." Soldiers in the right flank file stand fast with their left arms extended sideward with palms down, fingers and thumbs extended and joined. All other Soldiers turn to the left and double-time forward. After taking the sufficient number of steps, all Soldiers face the front and extend both arms sideward with palms down, fingers and thumbs extended and joined. The distance between fingertips is about 12 inches and dress is to the right.
- "ARMS DOWNWARD, *MOVE*." The Soldiers lower their arms smartly to their sides. Soldiers in the right flank file lower their left arms to their sides.
- "LEFT, *FACE*." Soldiers execute the left face.
- "EXTEND TO THE LEFT, *MARCH*." Soldiers in the right flank file stand fast with their left arms extended sideward with palms down, fingers and thumbs extended and joined. All other Soldiers turn to the left and double-time forward. After taking the sufficient number of steps, all Soldiers face the front and extend both arms sideward with palms down, fingers and thumbs extended and joined. The distance between fingertips is about 12 inches and dress is to the right.
- "ARMS DOWNWARD, *MOVE*." Soldiers lower their arms smartly to their sides. Soldiers in the right flank file lower their left arms to their sides.
- "RIGHT, *FACE*." Soldiers execute the right face.

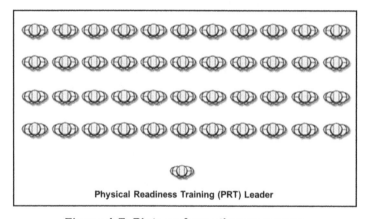

Figure 1-7. Platoon formation en masse

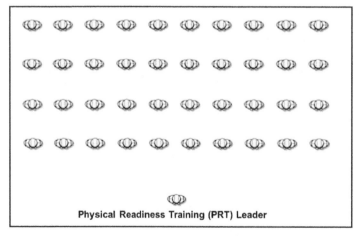

Figure 1-8. Platoon formation extended and covered

1-16. To reassemble the formation, the physical training leader commands, "ASSEMBLE TO THE RIGHT, *MARCH*." All Soldiers double-time to their original positions in the formation (see figure 1-7).

PREPARATION DRILLS

1-17. Physical training sessions always include drills that prepare the Soldier for the physical activity they are about to perform. Drills include the Preparation Drill, Four for the Core, Hip Stability Drill, Shoulder Stability Drill, Military Movement Drill, and Running Drill 1 through 5. Preparation Drills increase body heart rate and temperature, increase the flexibility of joints and muscles, and increase the responsiveness of nerves and muscles. When performed in a formation or collective setting, the principal instructor uses drill and ceremony techniques to lead the formation in cadence or timed exercises. Cadence is either slow or moderate (50 or 80 counts per minute, respectively). Assistant instructors maintain the ranks and ensure that Soldier perform the exercises precisely so as not to lose the training value of the drill.

1-18. In the Preparation Drill, each exercise is reverse-engineered from a combat-specific task. For example, the Bend and Reach prepares Soldiers to roll forward onto the ground, reach high overhead to climb, squat to take cover, reach to pick up ammunition, or check a fallen comrade. The Push-Up, with hands positioned under the shoulders, places the body into the optimal position to push an opponent away, push a disabled vehicle, and push up from the ground.

1-19. Returning the body to the Position of Attention between preparation exercises prevents overexertion, resets proper body position, and teaches Soldiers how to move to and from the ground without using their hands, replicating movement with their weapons. It allows leaders to check that their formations are paying attention to them—a core attribute of effective mental preparation for combat. Leaders can control the time between exercises to a minimum to increase the training effect. Cadence will always remain the same so that Soldiers have time to move through the fullest range of motion. If leaders maintain precision of movement, this approach increases time for the main activity of the session, increases the intensity of the preparation, and enhances the mental challenge.

1-20. Preparation Drill exercises may be further modified by performing fewer repetitions, selecting fewer exercises, or replacing some exercises with others. Table 1-1 includes three examples. This is appropriate when—

- There is condensed time to train.
- Soldiers require special conditioning.
- Activities are limited to only one of the physical readiness components—power, for instance.

Table 1-1. Three examples of a modified Preparation Drill

Preparation Drill (Standard)	Preparation Drill (Power-focused)	Preparation Drill (Condensed time)	Preparation Drill (Special conditioning)
Bend and reach 10 reps	Bend and reach 10 reps	Push-up 5 reps	Bend and reach (mod)
Rear lunge 10 reps	Squat bender, 10 reps	High jumper 10 reps	Rear lunge (mod)
High jumper 10 reps	Windmill 10 reps	Rower 10 reps	High jumper (mod)
Rower 10 reps	Forward lunge 10 reps	Prone row 5 reps	Rower (mod)
Squat bender 10 reps	Medial leg raise 5 reps	Rear lunge 5 reps	Squat bender (mod)
Bent-leg body twist 10 reps	Prone row 10 reps	Bent-leg body twist 5 reps	Bent-leg body twist (mod)
Forward lunge 10 reps	Single-leg tuck 5 reps		Forward lunge (mod)
Prone row 10 reps	Swimmer, 10 reps		Prone row (mod)
Windmill 10 reps			Windmill (mod)
Push-up 10 reps			Push-up (mod)
mod modified	reps repetitions	secs seconds	

1-21. After completing basic combat training, all graduated Soldiers perform ten repetitions of Preparation Drills and Conditioning Drills to standard. This fundamental level of physical readiness continues into the sustaining phase by repeated practice of the same drills and repetitions. The drills and repetitions form the foundation for peak performance in combat. Mastery of these drills and exercises guarantees very high levels of foundational fitness. Leaders who intend to demonstrate to new Soldiers that they know the physical training program also maintain proficiency in the drills and exercises. Soldiers in special conditioning have the same requirement to maintain fundamental skills. They perform modified versions of these exercises at speeds that are controlled, follow a standard, and encourage the fullest range of motion.

1-22. Leaders can develop other dynamic warm-up drills and exercises to take advantage of much greater equipment options and time available in the Holistic Health and Fitness (H2F) System. The goal of Preparation Drill is always the same—a total body, multi-planar series of low intensity, low impact movements that require Soldiers' movement skill and mental focus. Equipment modalities that support this goal include suspension systems, free weights, climbing racks, weight racks, resistance bands, and step-up boxes. Equipment that controls the movement for injured, deconditioned, or new Soldiers includes Endurance Training Machines (known as ETMs) and Strength Training Machines (known as STMs).

ACTIVITY DRILLS

1-23. Activities take up the majority of time in the physical training session. Table 1-2 summarizes physical training activities. See ATP 7-22.01 for Army Water Survival Training Exercises.

Table 1-2. Physical training activities

Drill	Description
Conditioning Drills 1/2/3	Moderate to advanced calisthenics that challenge core endurance, leg power, balance, and multi-planar coordination.
Climbing Drills 1 and 2	Off-ground, upper-body pulling exercises that incorporate core endurance and coordination.
Guerrilla Drill	Advanced movement skill exercises that require high levels of skill, confidence, and lower body strength.
Running Drills 1/2/3/4/5/6/7	Standardized exercises that improve perception of running as a skilled movement activity.
300-Meter Shuttle Run	Sprint drill that requires balance and coordination and advanced levels of anaerobic endurance.
30:60s and 60:120s	Timed sprint intervals at moderate to maximum speed that improve anaerobic endurance.
Release Run	A combination of formation- and own-pace running for time that aims for all Soldiers reaching the objective at the same time.
Terrain Run	Running on unimproved terrain for time that improves balance, coordination, and aerobic endurance.
Hill Run (Up and Down)	Interval running that provides advanced challenge to anaerobic endurance and leg speed.
Foot March	Sustained aerobic training that builds tolerance for dismounted operations.
Medicine Ball Drills 1 and 2	Total body resistance exercises that require hand-eye coordination, balance and muscular endurance.
Suspension Training Drills 1 and 2	On and off-ground pulling and core exercises that range from light to advanced challenge.
Landmine Drills 1 and 2	Moderate to heavy multi-planar resistance exercises that use a straight bar anchored to the ground.
Strength Training Circuit	A kettlebell circuit with movement drills separating 10 muscular endurance exercises each conducted for 1 minute.
Free Weight Core and Assistive	5 core and 13 assistive lifts of moderate to heavy resistance that maximizes muscular endurance, hypertrophy, power, and strength.
Pregnancy and Postpartum	Specific exercises for pregnant and postpartum Soldiers used in home programs, individual training, and collective training.
Army Water Survival Training	Training and test events that build proficiency in and around water while wearing the uniform and carrying equipment.

1-24. Typical features of activities during a training week include the following:

- Alternating days of strength and endurance activities.
- Avoidance of endurance activities on the same day as foot marches to control total foot time.
- Speed running at least once per week.
- Strength training that involves upper-body pushing and pulling, lower-body pushing and pulling, loaded carrying, and resisted-trunk rotation multiple times per week using more than body weight.
- Free-weight training on core lifts such as the Deadlift, Bench Press and Squat.
- Accessory lifts using Strength Training Machines and other resistive equipment such as medicine balls, suspension trainers, landmine apparatus and free weights.
- Daily sessions of 90–120 minutes.
- Foot marching under load.
- Practice or record Army Combat Fitness Test (ACFT) on Monday or after another extended period of recovery or taper.

RECOVERY DRILLS

1-25. The two drills used for recovery, coupled with proper nutrition and sleep, carry over to the next physical training session. Proper recovery results in positive adaptation to the stress of training, maintains alertness, and improves the Soldier's ability to progress in the readiness training program using—

- The Recovery Drill (known as RD) that gradually and safely tapers off activities to bring the body back to its pre-exercise state. Recovery continues throughout the day with active nutrition and sleep practices.
- Preventive Maintenance Checks and Services (known as PMCS) that is a self-check and fix for musculoskeletal issues. It provides early identification of issues so that Soldiers can take care of issues before they become chronic or severe.

This page intentionally left blank.

Chapter 2
Positions and Grips

2-1.   When Soldiers are training in formations, Soldiers assume the proper starting position for each exercise on the command, "STARTING POSITION, *MOVE*." When conducting exercises, leaders command Soldiers to return to the Position of Attention from the final position of the exercise. Moving in and out of these positions challenges mobility and gives Soldiers and their H2F leaders information that they in turn can use to improve physical readiness. See figure 2-1 for all the positions.

Figure 2-1. Positions

SQUAT

2-2.   The Squat position is a transitional position reached when moving to and from the ground. It promotes flexibility in the spine, hips, knees, and ankles in preparation for controlled movement to the ground. From the Position of Attention, start the movement to the squat position. Lower the body by bending the knees and placing the hands on the ground between the knees. Arms will be between the knees. Heels may be off the ground so that the body weight is distributed between the balls of the feet and the hands. Reverse these steps when moving from the ground to return to the Position of Attention. Figure 2-2 on page 2-2 illustrates the Squat position.

Figure 2-2. Squat position

FRONT LEANING REST

2-3.   The Front Leaning Rest promotes stability in the shoulders, trunk, and hips in preparation for controlled movement to the ground. The Front Leaning Rest is the resting position for the Hand-Release Push-Up in the ACFT. Soldiers use this position to train their body's transition to and from the ground. From the Squat Position, start the movement to the Front Leaning Rest. After shifting the body weight from the feet to the hands, thrust both feet rearwards, landing with the feet together. The Soldier should control the hips so that they do not dip to the ground when the feet land. From the heels to the top of the head, the body should form a straight line. This is the standard position of rest during the Hand-Release Push-Up (known as HRP)—the index finger is inside the outside edge of the shoulder. Figure 2-3 illustrates the front leaning rest position.

SIX-POINT STANCE

2-4.   The Six-Point Stance is a modified position for the Front Leaning Rest. From the Front Leaning Rest, assume the Six-Point Stance by dropping the knees to the ground and pointing the toes to the rear. Figure 2-4 demonstrates the Six-Point Stance position.

Figure 2-3. Front Leaning Rest position

Figure 2-4. Six-Point Stance position

STRADDLE STANCE

2-5.   The Straddle Stance is the preparatory position for many physical readiness training exercises. Assume the Straddle Stance by standing with the feet directed ahead and shoulder-width apart. Figure 2-5 illustrates the Straddle Stance position.

FORWARD LEANING STANCE

2-6.   The Forward Leaning Stance is the preparatory position for the High Jumper exercise. Assume the Forward Leaning Stance by standing with the feet straight ahead and aligned beneath the shoulders. Bend forward 45 degrees at the waist with the knees bent to 45 degrees. Keep the back straight, maintaining a straight line from the head to the hips. Figure 2-6 demonstrates the Forward Leaning Stance position.

Figure 2-5. Straddle Stance position

Figure 2-6. The Forward Leaning Stance position

PRONE

2-7.   The Prone position is the starting position for the Hand-Release Push-Up and for transitioning to and from the ground. Assume the Prone position by lowering the body to the ground from the Front Leaning Rest position. Feet are together or up to a boot's width apart, hands remain on the ground beneath the shoulders. Figure 2-7 on page 2-4 shows the Prone position.

SUPINE

2-8.   The Supine position is the transition position for certain exercises conducted on the ground. Movement into and out of the Supine position is a skill required for conducting supine exercises on the ground and for hands-free movement from the ground. From the Straddle Stance, move one foot to the rear while slowly lowering the body until the rear knee touches the ground. This is the Half-Kneeling position. From the Half-Kneeling position, sweep the rear leg under the body while sitting back onto the buttocks. The hands remain off the ground during the movement. Straighten both legs so that they are placed out front and together on the ground.

2-9.   To complete the movement to the Supine position, lay back onto the ground so that the legs and body are aligned with arms and hands held close to the body. Figure 2-8 on page 2-4 illustrates the Supine position.

Figure 2-7. Prone position

Figure 2-8. Supine position

2-10. If the Soldier has difficulty moving into or out of the Supine position, he or she may place both hands on the ground on the same side of the body to support the movement.

HALF-KNEELING

2-11. From the Straddle Stance, move one foot to the rear while slowly lowering the body until the rear knee touches the ground. This is the Half-Kneeling position. Figure 2-9 shows the Half-Kneeling position.

SITTING

2-12. The Sitting position is the transition position for certain exercises conducted on the ground. Assume the Sitting position from the Half-Kneeling position by sweeping the rear leg under the body while sitting back onto the buttocks. The hands remain off the ground during the movement. Straighten both legs so that they are placed together on the ground. Figure 2-10 illustrates the Sitting position. In order to support the body weight, both hands will be placed on the ground next to the hips, fingers facing forwards.

Figure 2-9. Half-Kneeling position

Figure 2-10. Sitting position

GRIPS

2-13. Paragraphs 2-14 through 2-20 include the names and descriptions of the various grips that Soldiers use when they are weight training. Figure 2-11 illustrates the different grips.

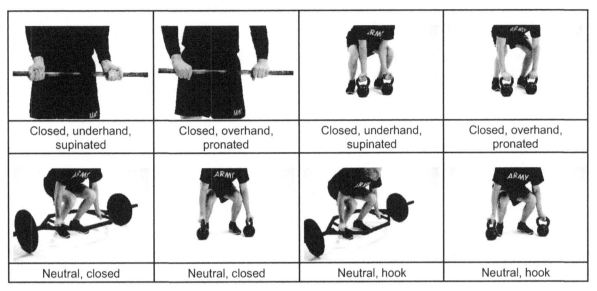

Closed, underhand, supinated	Closed, overhand, pronated	Closed, underhand, supinated	Closed, overhand, pronated
Neutral, closed	Neutral, closed	Neutral, hook	Neutral, hook

Figure 2-11. Grips

CLOSED

2-14. The closed grip or composite grip requires that Soldiers wrap their thumb around the bar in the opposite direction to their fingers. The thumb normally overlaps with the fingers. Occasionally they tuck the thumb beneath the fingers to form a hook grip.

OPEN

2-15. The open or false grip is used on selectorized machines when there is no risk of the bar rolling off the hand causing the weight to be dropped. It is not a safe grip for use on Climbing Drill or Free Weight Training exercises.

UNDERHAND

2-16. With the underhand or supinated grip, Soldiers turn their forearms and hands out so that their palms face away from the body when initially gripping a bar.

OVERHAND

2-17. With the overhand or pronated grip, Soldiers turn their forearms and hands in so that the palms face toward the body when initially gripping a bar.

NEUTRAL

2-18. The neutral grip is used to lift the hex bar and when carrying a kettlebell in each hand for the Forward Lunge—the third exercise in the Strength Training Circuit.

HOOK

2-19. The closed grip or composite grip requires that the thumb wraps around the bar in the opposite direction to the fingers. The thumb normally overlaps with the fingers. When the thumb tucks beneath the fingers this is called a hook grip.

ALTERNATING GRIP

2-20. The alternating grip is used with a straight bar and is sometimes referred to as a mixed grip. One hand is supinated and the other is pronated. The Alternating Grip Pull-Up and Leg Tuck exercises use a grip where both hands are pronated, palms facing which holds the Soldier perpendicular to the bar, similar to the grip and position used in rope traversing and rope climbing.

Chapter 3

Preparation Drills

THE PREPARATION DRILL

3-1.   The Preparation Drill (known as PD) is a series of exercises intended to decrease the likelihood of suffering a musculoskeletal injury during the execution of more rigorous physical training such as the ACFT. The Preparation Drill is composed of 10 exercises: Bend and Reach, Rear Lunge, High Jumper, Rower, Squat Bender, Windmill, Forward Lunge, Prone Row, Bent-Leg Body Twist, and Push-Up.

3-2.   Videos of H2F test events and exercises located on the Central Army Registry website at https://atiam.train.army.mil/catalog/search?current=true&filetype=mp4&respect_date=5%2F1%2F2020&search_terms=CIMT demonstrate movements. (Copy and paste this address after accessing the Central Army Registry website if the demonstrations do not populate.) Additional support for H2F test events and exercises are located on the Army Combat Fitness Test website at https://www.army.mil/acft/.

1. BEND AND REACH

3-3.   The Bend and Reach (see figure 3-1) is the first exercise in the Preparation Drill. By flexing the trunk, hips, and knees, and extending the shoulders, the Bend and Reach prepares the Soldier for more vigorous activity such as squatting, rolling, and climbing. Soldiers conduct the movement in formation at a slow cadence:

- The starting position for the Bend and Reach is the Straddle Stance position with the arms overhead, elbows fully extended, palms facing inward, fingers and thumbs extended and joined.
- On count 1, move from the starting position into a partial squat with the heels remaining on the ground. Round the spine to allow the arms to reach as far as possible between the legs. The neck flexes to tuck the chin and head and to allow the Soldier to look to the rear.
- On count 2, return to the starting position.
- On count 3, repeat count 1.
- On count 4, return to the starting position.

Figure 3-1. PD1 Bend and Reach

2. REAR LUNGE

3-4.   The Rear Lunge (see figure 3-2 and figure 3-3) is the second exercise in the Preparation Drill. This exercise promotes flexibility, strength, and balance in the hip and leg. It prepares the Soldier for taking cover and assuming kneeling firing positions. Soldiers conduct the movement in formation at a slow cadence:

- The starting position for the Rear Lunge is the Straddle Stance position with hands on hips.
- On count 1, keeping hands on hips, take an exaggerated step backwards with the left leg, touching down with the ball of the foot placed directly back from the starting position. The heel should be off the ground, and a stretch should be felt in the front of the left hip and thigh. If not, allow the body to continue to lower to increase flexibility.
- On count 2, return to the starting position, maintaining the same distance between the feet as used in the Straddle Stance.
- On count 3, repeat count 1 with the right leg.
- On count 4, return to the starting position.

Figure 3-2. PD2 Rear Lunge

Figure 3-3. PD2 Proper technique to execute the Rear Lunge

3. HIGH JUMPER

3-5. The High Jumper (see figure 3-4) is the third exercise in the Preparation Drill. This exercise promotes correct jumping, landing, balance, and coordination, and it prepares the Soldier to build explosive strength. Soldiers conduct the movement in formation at a moderate cadence:

- The starting position for the High Jumper is the Forward Leaning Stance, palms facing inwards, fingers and thumbs extended and joined.
- On count 1, swing the arms forward until they are parallel to the ground. At the same time, jump a few inches vertically.
- On count 2, land softly on the balls of the feet and return to the starting position. Maintain the same distance between the feet as during the Forward Leaning Stance.
- On count 3, swing the arms vigorously forward and overhead to unweight the upper body. At the same time, jump forcefully straight up from the ground.
- On count 4, land softly on the balls of the feet and return to the starting position.

Figure 3-4. PD3 High Jumper

4. ROWER

3-6.   The Rower (see figure 3-5 and figure 3-6) is the fourth exercise in the Preparation Drill. This exercise improves abdominal strength and total body coordination. It prepares the Soldier to move from the Supine to Sitting positions and exercises in Conditioning Drills and Climbing Drills.

3-7.   Soldiers conduct the movement at a slow cadence:

- The starting position for the Rower is the Supine position with arms overhead, feet together and pointing up. The head is 1–2 inches off the ground to work muscles in the front of the neck. Arms are overhead with hands at shoulder width, palms facing inward with fingers and thumbs extended and joined.
- On count 1, sit up while bending at the hip and knees and swinging arms forward until they are parallel to the ground. At the end of this count, the feet are flat on the ground with knees positioned between the arms. The arms are parallel to the ground.
- On count 2, reverse the movement performed in count 1 to return to the starting position.
- On count 3, repeat count 1.
- On count 4, return to the starting position.
- Perform 5–10 repetitions.

Figure 3-5. PD4 Rower

Figure 3-6. PD4 Proper technique to execute the Rower

5. SQUAT BENDER

3-8. The Squat Bender (see figure 3-7) is the fifth exercise in the Preparation Drill. This exercise develops strength, endurance, and flexibility in the lower back and thigh muscles. It prepares Soldiers to use proper lifting technique in more vigorous training and testing events that require heavy lifts. Soldiers conduct the movement at a slow cadence:

- The starting position for the Squat Bender is the Straddle Stance position with hands on hips.
- On count 1, squat while leaning slightly forward from the waist, keeping the head up and moving both arms to a position in front of the body and parallel to the ground. Palms face inwards.
- On count 2, reverse the movement performed in count 1 to return to the starting position.
- On count 3, with the knees slightly bent, bend forward at the waist. Maintain the head in alignment with the spine and keep the spine straight. Reach toward the ground until a stretch is felt in the back of the thighs.
- On count 4, return to the starting position.
- Perform 5–10 repetitions.

Figure 3-7. PD5 Squat Bender

6. WINDMILL

3-9.   The Windmill (see figure 3-8 and figure 3-9) is the sixth exercise in the Preparation Drill. This exercise develops the ability to safely bend and simultaneously rotate the trunk. It requires flexibility in the spine and coordination of the shoulder girdle. It prepares Soldiers to use proper movement technique in more vigorous training, testing, and combat tasks. Soldiers conduct the movement at a slow cadence:

- The starting position for the Windmill is the Straddle Stance position with arms straight out to the side. Fingers and thumbs are extended and joined, palms are facing down.
- On count 1, bend the hips and knees while rotating the trunk to the left. Reach down to touch the outside of the left foot with the right hand and look to the rear. The left arm is pulled rearward to maintain alignment across the shoulders with the right arm.
- On count 2, reverse the movement performed in count 1 to return to the starting position.
- On count 3, repeat count 1, this time to the right.
- On count 4, return to the starting position.
- Perform 5–10 repetitions.

Figure 3-8. PD6 Windmill

Figure 3-9. PD6 Proper technique to execute the Windmill

7. FORWARD LUNGE

3-10. The Forward Lunge (see figure 3-10) is the seventh exercise in the Preparation Drill. This exercise develops balance and leg strength. It prepares Soldiers to use proper movement technique to perform lifts such as a litter carry. Soldiers conduct the movement at a slow cadence:

- The starting position for the Forward Lunge is the Straddle Stance position with hands on hips.
- On count 1, take a step forward with the left leg until the left heel is 3–6 inches ahead of the right foot. At the same time, bend at the hips and knees to lunge forward, keeping the back straight. Do not look down and do not bring the feet closer together.
- On count 2, reverse the movement performed in count 1 to return to the starting position.
- On count 3, repeat count 1, this time stepping forward with the right foot.

Figure 3-10. PD7 Forward Lunge

8. PRONE ROW

3-11. The Prone Row is the eighth exercise in the Preparation Drill (see figure 3-11). This exercise develops the strength of the neck, upper back, and shoulders. It prepares Soldiers to fire from the Prone position and to tolerate the weight of the helmet and body armor across the shoulders and neck. Soldiers conduct the movement at a slow cadence:

- The starting position for the Prone Row is the Prone position with arms overhead, palms down, fingers and thumbs extended and joined. Arms are lifted 1–2 inches from the ground and toes are pointed to the rear.
- On count 1, raise the head and chest slightly while lifting the arms and pulling them rearward. Make hands into fists as they move toward the shoulders.
- Feet stay together and on the ground. Arms and hands are off the ground.
- On count 2, reverse the movement performed in count 1 to return to the starting position. Arms and hands remain off the ground.
- On count 3, repeat count 1.

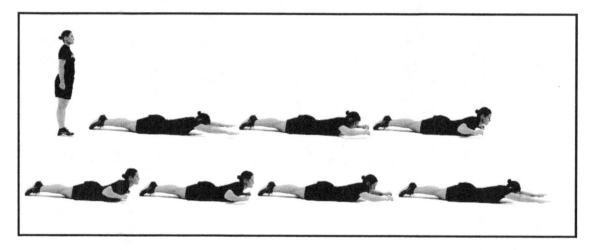

Figure 3-11. PD8 Prone Row

9. BENT-LEG BODY TWIST

3-12. The Bent-Leg Body Twist is the ninth exercise in the Preparation Drill (see figure 3-12). This exercise strengthens the trunk and hip muscles while promoting control of trunk rotation. It is a safe way to prepare for loaded trunk movements in more vigorous training, testing and combat tasks. Soldiers conduct the movement at a slow cadence:

- The starting position for the Bent-Leg Body Twist is the Supine position with the hips and knees bent to 90 degrees, arms straight out to the side, palms on the ground. The knees and feet are together.
- On count 1, rotate the legs to the left while keeping the upper back and arms in place on the ground. The legs drop together toward the ground.
- On count 2, reverse the movement performed in count 1 to return to the starting position.
- On count 3, repeat count 1, this time rotating the legs to the right.
- On count 4, return to the starting position.

10. PUSH-UP

3-13. The Push-Up is the final exercise in the Preparation Drill (see figure 3-13). This exercise strengthens the muscles of the chest, shoulders, arms, and trunk. When conducted to standard, it is a safe way to prepare for more vigorous pushing motions required in training, testing, and combat tasks. Soldiers conduct the movement at a moderate cadence:

- The starting position for the Push-Up is the Front Leaning Rest. Hands are directly beneath the shoulders with fingers spread. Feet are together. The body forms a straight line from the top of the head to the heels. Soldiers maintain this position throughout the exercise.
- On count 1, bend the elbows, lowering the body until the upper arms are parallel to the ground.
- On count 2, reverse the movement performed in count 1 to return to the starting position.
- On count 3, repeat count 1.

Figure 3-12. PD9 Bent-Leg Body Twist

Figure 3-13. PD10 Push-Up

PREPARATION DRILL (MODIFIED) (PD MOD)

3-14. Each physical training exercise may be modified to accommodate a variety of physical limitations. By following their individual DA Form 3349 (*Physical Profile*) and the principle of progression, Soldiers can gradually re-condition themselves to the standard range of motion and repetitions required for a full return to duty. Soldiers who know the standard for each exercise can modify it in more ways than this publication can illustrate. When an exercise cannot be performed at all (it is restricted on the DA Form 3349), the Soldier selects an alternative exercise with the same cadence that requires similar movements or muscle groups. In formation, he or she can perform the alternative exercise, modifying as necessary, but using the same cadence as the rest of the formation.

1. BEND AND REACH (MODIFIED)

3-15. The Bend and Reach (see figure 3-14) may be modified by decreasing the range of motion of the spine and the squat, and by limiting the use of one or both arms. Figure 3-14 gives one example of the modified movement Soldiers conduct at a slow cadence:

- The starting position for the modified Bend and Reach is the Straddle Stance position with hands on hips.
- On count 1, move from the starting position into a partial squat with the heels remaining on the ground. Lean forward at the waist, keeping the spine straight and reaching to the ground with straight arms.
- On count 2, return to the starting position.
- On count 3, repeat count 1.
- On count 4, return to the starting position.

2. REAR LUNGE (MODIFIED)

3-16. The Rear Lunge (see figure 3-15) may be modified by decreasing the range of motion of the lunge and knee bend, by stepping back with only one leg, or by widening or narrowing the stance. Figure 3-15 gives one example of the modified movement Soldiers conduct at a slow cadence:

- On count 1, keeping hands on hips, take a step backwards with the left or right leg. Touch down with the ball of the foot placed directly back from the starting position or wider to improve balance. The heel may be on the ground. Lower the body into the lunge position while controlling the knee bend.
- On count 2, return to the starting position maintaining the same distance between the feet as used in the Straddle Stance.
- On count 3, repeat count 1 with the right or left leg.
- On count 4, return to the starting position. Over several repetitions, or physical training sessions, progress to a deeper rear lunge.

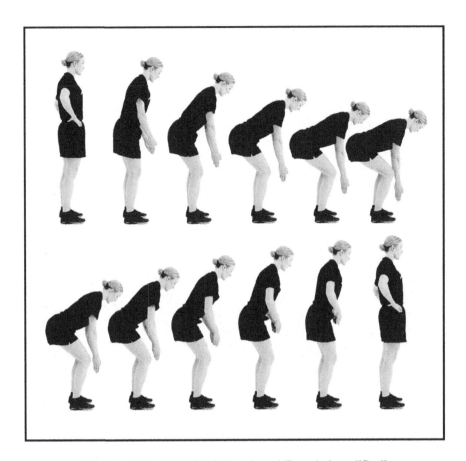

Figure 3-14. PD MOD1 Bend and Reach (modified)

Figure 3-15. PD MOD2 Rear Lunge (modified)

3. HIGH JUMPER (MODIFIED)

3-17. The High Jumper may be modified by decreasing the range of motion of one or both arms, the height of the jumps, and the cadence. Figure 3-16 gives one example of the modified movement Soldiers conduct by changing the standard moderate cadence to slow:

- The starting position for the modified High Jumper is the Forward Leaning Stance with a reduced squat, palms facing inwards, and fingers and thumbs extended and joined.
- On count 1, swing the arms forward until they are parallel to the ground. At the same time lift the heels off the ground a few inches without jumping.
- On count 3, swing the arms as far overhead as possible. At the same time lift the heels off the ground a few inches without jumping.
- On count 4, return to the starting position by lowering the heels back to the floor.

Figure 3-16. PD MOD3 High Jumper (modified)

4. ROWER (MODIFIED)

3-18. The Rower may be modified by decreasing the use of one or both arms, decreasing the use of one or both legs, or by decreasing the range of trunk flexion, and by keeping the head on the ground. Figure 3-17 on page 3-14 gives one example of the modified movement Soldiers conduct at a slow cadence:

- The starting position for the modified Rower is the Supine position with arms crossed over the chest, knees flexed, and head resting on the ground.
- On count 1, sit up or and reach to the knees.
- On count 2, reverse the movement performed in count 1 to return to the starting position.
- On count 3, repeat count 1.
- On count 4, return to the starting position.

Figure 3-17. PD MOD4 Rower (modified)

5. SQUAT BENDER (MODIFIED)

3-19. The Squat Bender can be modified by reducing the motion of the knee and trunk flexion and by reducing movement of the arms. Figure 3-18 on page 3-14 gives one example of the modified movement Soldiers conduct at a slow cadence:

- The starting position for the modified Squat Bender is the Straddle Stance position with hands on hips.
- On count 1, squat slightly while leaning forward from the waist, keeping the head up and moving one or both arms toward the knees. Palms face inwards.
- On count 2, reverse the movement performed in count 1 to return to the starting position.
- On count 3, repeat count 1, attempting to progress the range of motion of the trunk, arms, and legs.
- On count 4, return to the starting position.

Figure 3-18. PD MOD5 Squat Bender (modified)

6. WINDMILL (MODIFIED)

3-20. The modified Windmill has two alternatives. The starting position for the modified Windmill is the Straddle Stance. Figure 3-19 illustrates the first alternative with hands on hips. Figure 3-20 shows the second alternative with arms straight out to the sides at 90 degrees to the trunk. Soldiers conduct the exercise at a slow cadence:

- On count 1, bend the hips and knees while rotating the trunk to the left. Reach down to touch the outside of the left foot with the right hand and look to the rear. The left arm stays in its starting position, with hand on hip. Alternatively, with arms out to the side, rotate the trunk to the left, avoiding any hip or knee flexion.
- On count 2, reverse the movement performed in count 1 to return to the starting position.
- On count 3, repeat count 1, this time to the right.
- On count 4, return to the starting position.

Figure 3-19. PD MOD6 Windmill (modified)

Figure 3-20. PD MOD6 Windmill (modified) alternative movement

7. FORWARD LUNGE (MODIFIED)

3-21. The Forward Lunge can be modified by decreasing the range of motion, keeping the feet closer together, or moving just one foot. Figure 3-21 shows one example of the modified movement Soldiers conduct at a slow cadence:

- The starting position for the modified Forward Lunge is the Straddle Stance position with hands on hips.
- On count 1, take a step forward with the left or right leg until the forward heel is 3–6 inches ahead of the rear foot. At the same time, bend at the hips and knees to lunge forward, keeping the back straight. Bring the feet closer together if necessary.
- On count 2, reverse the movement performed in count 1 to return to the starting position.
- On count 3, repeat count 1, switching foot movement.
- On count 4, return to the starting position.

Figure 3-21. PD MOD7 Forward Lunge (modified)

8. PRONE ROW (MODIFIED)

3-22. The Prone Row may be modified by decreasing the range of motion of the arms, moving only one arm to standard (see figure 3-22), or by performing the arm movements while remaining standing using the starting position for the Bend and Reach (see figure 3-23). Soldiers conduct the standing version of the modification at a slow cadence:

- The starting position is the same as the Bend and Reach, arms overhead, palms forward, fingers and thumbs extended and joined.
- On count 1, raise the chin, head and chest slightly while moving the arms down to the sides of the trunk while flexing the elbows. Make the hands into fists as they move toward the shoulders.

- On count 2, return to the starting position.
- On count 3, repeat count 1.
- On count 4, return to the starting position.

Figure 3-22. PD MOD8 Prone Row (modified)

Figure 3-23. PD MOD8 Prone Row (modified) alternative movement

9. BENT-LEG BODY TWIST (MODIFIED)

3-23. The Bent-Leg Body Twist can be modified by changing the arm position, resting the head on the ground, keeping the feet on the ground, reducing the range of rotation, and by moving only one leg from the starting position. Figure 3-24 on page 3-18 gives one example of the modified movement Soldiers conduct at a slow cadence:

- The starting position for the modified Bent-Leg Body Twist is the Supine position with head on the ground, arms at 45 degrees from the trunk, hips and knees bent with feet on the ground. The knees and feet are together.
- On count 1, rotate the legs to the left while keeping the upper back and arms in place on the ground. The legs drop together toward the ground.
- On count 2, reverse the movement performed in count 1 to return to the starting position.

Figure 3-24. PD MOD9 Bent-Leg Body Twist (modified)

10. PUSH-UP (MODIFIED)

3-24. The Push-Up can be modified by moving to the Six-Point Stance position. This modified exercise limits the range of motion and weight on the ankles, shoulders, arms, and wrists (see figure 3-25). Soldiers conduct the movement at a moderate cadence:

- The starting position for the modified Push-Up is the Six-Point Stance position. Hands are directly beneath the shoulders with fingers spread. The body forms a straight line from the head to the knees. Feet point to the rear.
- On count 2, return to the starting position. If necessary, reduce the range of motion of the elbow to accommodate for the injury.
- On count 3, repeat count 1, reducing the range of motion if necessary.
- On count 4, return to the starting position.

Figure 3-25. PD MOD10 Push-Up (modified)

Chapter 4

Stability Drills

HIP STABILITY DRILL (HSD)

4-1. The Hip Stability Drill (known as HSD) consists of five exercises designed to improve the flexibility and muscular endurance of the leg and hip muscles. The Hip Stability Drill exercises are the Lateral Leg Raise, Medial Leg Raise, Bent-Leg Lateral Raise, Single-Leg Tuck, and Single Leg Over.

4-2. Demonstration videos of stability drills are located on the Central Army Registry website at https://atiam.train.army.mil/catalog/search?current=true&filetype=mp4&respect_date=5%2F1%2F2020&search_terms=CIMT. (Copy and paste this address after accessing the Central Army Registry website if the demonstrations do not populate.) Additional support for H2F test events and exercises are located on Army Combat Fitness Test website at https://www.army.mil/acft/.

1. LATERAL LEG RAISE

4-3. Figure 4-1 illustrates the Lateral Leg Raise. Soldiers conduct it in formation at a slow cadence:

- The starting position for the Lateral Leg Raise is the Sitting position. Soldiers move to a right side-lying position, with legs extended together, left leg on top of the right. Support trunk off the ground with the right elbow. Bend the elbow to 90 degrees and place it directly below the shoulder. Make a fist with the right hand and rest it on the ground, thumb up. Place the left hand across the stomach.
- On the count of 1, raise the left leg a short distance above the right leg. Control the movement to the end point where the left foot will be 6–8 inches above the right foot.
- On count 2, return to the starting position.
- On count 3, repeat count 1.
- On count 4, return to the first starting position.
- Repeat 5–10 times.
- On the command, "CHANGE POSITION, *MOVE*," swing the legs toward the front of the formation, swiveling on the buttocks into the second starting position—the left side-lying position—with the trunk supported on the left elbow.
- Complete the same series of repetitions with the right leg and hip.

Figure 4-1. HSD1 Lateral Leg Raise

2. MEDIAL LEG RAISE

4-4.   The second exercise in the Hip Stability Drill is the Medial Leg Raise. Figure 4-2 shows Soldiers performing the exercise in a formation at a slow cadence:

- The starting position for the Medial Leg Raise is the Sitting position. Soldiers move to the left side lying position, with the left leg extended and the right leg bent at the knees and rotated so that the right foot rests on the ground behind the left knee, foot pointing away from the body.
- Support the trunk off the ground with the left elbow. Bend the elbow to 90 degrees, placing it directly below the shoulder. Make the left hand in a fist and rest it on the ground, thumb up. Place the right hand across the stomach.
- On count 1, raise the left leg a short distance from the ground. Control the movement to the end point where the left foot will be 6 to 8 inches above the ground.
- On count 2, return to the starting position.
- On count 3, repeat count 1.
- On count 4, return to the first starting position.
- Repeat 5 to 10 times.
- On the command, "CHANGE POSITION, *MOVE*," swing the legs toward the front of the formation, swiveling on the buttocks into the second starting position with the trunk supported on the right elbow.
- Complete the same series of repetitions for the right leg and hip.

Figure 4-2. HSD2 Medial Leg Raise

3. BENT-LEG LATERAL RAISE

4-5.   The third exercise in the Hip Stability Drill is the Bent-Leg Lateral Raise. Figure 4-3 illustrates the exercise Soldiers perform it in a formation at a slow cadence:

- The starting position for the Bent-Leg Lateral Raise is the Sitting position. Soldiers move to a side-lying position, with legs together, knees bent to 90 degrees and, left leg on top of the right. The thighs and trunk form a straight line.
- Support the trunk off the ground with the right elbow. Bend the elbow to 90 degrees, and place it directly below the shoulder. Fist the right hand and rest it on the ground, thumb up. Place the left hand across the stomach.
- On count 1, raise the left knee a short distance above the right leg. Feet remain together. Control the movement to the end point where the left knee will be 6–8 inches above the right knee.
- On count 2, return to the starting position.
- On count 3, repeat count 1
- On count 4, return to the first starting position.

- Repeat 5–10 times.
- On the command, "CHANGE POSITION, *MOVE*," swing the legs toward the front of the formation, swiveling on the buttocks into the second starting position with the trunk supported on the left elbow.

Figure 4-3. HSD3 Bent-Leg Lateral Raise

4. SINGLE-LEG TUCK

4-6.   The Single-Leg Tuck is the fourth exercise in the Hip Stability Drill. Figure 4-4 on page 4-4 shows the exercise Soldiers perform it in a formation at a slow cadence:

- The starting position for the Single-Leg Tuck is the Sitting position. Soldiers move to a side lying position, with legs extended, the left leg is held 6–8 inches above the right.
- Support the trunk off the ground with the right elbow. Bend the elbow to 90 degrees and place it directly below the shoulder. Fist the right hand and rest it on the ground, thumb up. Place the left hand across the stomach.
- On the count of 1, bend the left knee and hip to 90 degrees, holding the leg and foot in the same plane throughout the movement. Control the movement to the end point. The left foot and knee should be the same height from the ground to work the correct muscles in the hip. Do not let the foot drop to the ground.
- On count 2, return to the starting position.
- On count 3, repeat count 1.
- On count 4, return to the first starting position.
- Repeat 5–10 times.
- On the command, "CHANGE POSITION, *MOVE*," swing the legs together toward the front of the formation, swiveling on the buttocks into the second starting position with the trunk supported on the left elbow.
- Complete the same series of repetitions for the right leg and hip.

Figure 4-4. HSD4 Single-Leg Tuck

5. SINGLE LEG OVER

4-7.   The Single Leg Over is the fifth exercise in the Hip Stability Drill (see figure 4-5). This exercise develops flexibility of the hip and low back. Soldiers conduct the movement in formation for 30–60 seconds.

- The starting position for the Single Leg Over is the Supine position with arms straight out to the side on ground with palms down with fingers and thumbs extended and joined. Feet are together on the ground. The head is on the ground.
- On the command "READY, *STRETCH*," bend the left knee to 90 degrees over the right leg and grasp the outside of the left knee with the right hand pulling toward the right. Keep the left shoulder and arm on the ground. Hold this position for 20–30 seconds.
- On the command "STARTING POSITION, *MOVE*," assume the starting position.
- On the command "CHANGE POSITION, READY, *STRETCH*," bend the right knee to 90 degrees over the left leg and grasp the outside of the right knee with the left hand pulling toward the left. Keep the right shoulder and arm on the ground. Hold this position for 20–30 seconds.
- On the command "STARTING POSITION, *MOVE*," return to the starting position, and then the Position of Attention.

SHOULDER STABILITY DRILL (SSD)

4-8.   The Shoulder Stability Drill is designed to develop strength and stability in the shoulder muscles. Soldiers can perform this drill throughout their career. It improves foundational readiness for more rigorous training and combat tasks that involve carrying, climbing, pulling, and pushing. In paragraphs 4-9 through 4-12, each illustration features another Soldier providing feedback to aid in proper execution of the exercise. In the H2F system, the use of coaching, training, and battle buddy input is highly encouraged.

1. I RAISE

4-9.   The first exercise for the Shoulder Stability Drill is the I Raise (see figure 4-6). Soldiers perform the exercise in a formation at a slow cadence:

- The starting position for the I Raise is the Prone position with arms laying parallel to each other on the ground above the head. This is the I position. The head is slightly elevated. Feet are together and toes are pointing rearward. Fingers and thumbs are extended and joined with palms facing each other.
- On the count of 1, raise both arms from the ground 3–6 inches while continuing to keep the elbows straight. The head remains in its starting position.
- On count 2, return to the starting position.
- On count 3, repeat count 1.
- On count 4, return to the starting position.

Figure 4-5. HSD5 Single Leg Over

Figure 4-6. SSD1 I Raise

2. T RAISE

4-10. The second exercise for the Shoulder Stability Drill is the T Raise. Figure 4-7 illustrates the exercise as performed in a formation at a slow cadence:

- The starting position for the T Raise is the Prone position with arms laying on the ground straight out from the shoulders at 90 degrees to the trunk. This is the T position. The head is slightly elevated. Feet are together and toes are pointing rearward. Fingers and thumbs are extended and joined with palms perpendicular to the ground, facing directly ahead.
- On the count of 1, raise both arms from the ground 3–6 inches while continuing to keep the elbows straight. The head remains in its starting position.
- On count 2, return to the starting position.
- On count 3, repeat count 1.
- On count 4, return to the starting position.

Figure 4-7. SSD2 T raise

3. Y RAISE

4-11. The third exercise for the Shoulder Stability Drill is the Y Raise. Figure 4-8 shows Soldiers performing the exercise in a formation at a slow cadence:

- The starting position for the Y Raise is the Prone position with arms laying on the ground extended overhead at 45 degrees to the trunk. This is the Y position. The head is slightly elevated. Feet are together and toes are pointing rearward. Fingers and thumbs are extended and joined with palms facing each other.
- On the count of 1, raise both arms from the ground 3–6 inches while continuing to keep the elbows straight. The head remains in its starting position.
- On count 2, return to the starting position.
- On count 3, repeat count 1.
- On count 4, return to the starting position.

Figure 4-8. SSD3 Y Raise

4. L RAISE

4-12. The fourth exercise for the Shoulder Stability Drill is the L Raise. Figure 4-9 shows Soldiers perform the exercise in a formation at a slow cadence:

- The starting position for the L Raise is the Prone position with arms laying on the ground straight out to the side at 90 degrees to the trunk and elbows bent to 90 degrees. Hands are at head level with palms facing the head. This is the L position. The head is slightly elevated. Feet are together and toes are pointing rearward. Fingers and thumbs are extended and joined with palms facing each other.
- On the count of 1, raise both arms from the ground 3–6 inches while continuing to keep the elbows bent. The head remains in its starting position. The elbows, forearms, and hands should leave the ground at the same time.
- On count 2, return to the starting position.
- On count 3, repeat count 1.
- On count 4, return to the starting position.

Figure 4-9. SSD4 L Raise

5. W RAISE

4-13. The fifth exercise for the Shoulder Stability Drill is the W Raise. Figures 4-10 and 4-11 show the exercise as performed in a formation at a slow cadence:

- The starting position for the W Raise is the Prone position with arms on the ground at 45 degrees to the trunk and elbows bent to 45 degrees. This is the W position. The head is slightly elevated. Feet are together and toes are pointing rearward. Fingers and thumbs are extended and joined with palms facing each other.
- On the count of 1, raise both arms from the ground 3–6 inches while continuing to keep the elbows bent. The head remains in its starting position. The elbows, forearms, and hands should leave the ground at the same time.
- On count 2, return to the starting position.
- On count 3, repeat count 1.
- On count 4, return to the starting position.

Figure 4-10. SSD5 W Raise with improper form

Figure 4-11. SSD5 W Raise

Chapter 5

Conditioning Drills

CONDITIONING DRILL 1 (CD1)

5-1. Conditioning Drill 1 (known as CD1) consists of five exercises designed to improve muscular strength and endurance as well as balance and coordination. The Conditioning Drill 1 consists of the following exercises: Power Jump, V-Up, Mountain Climber, Leg-Tuck and Twist, and Single-Leg Push-Up.

5-2. Demonstration videos of Conditioning Drills are located on the Central Army Registry website at https://atiam.train.army.mil/catalog/search?current=true&filetype=mp4&respect_date=5%2F1%2F2020&search_terms=CIMT. (Copy and paste this address after accessing the Central Army Registry website if the demonstrations do not populate.) Additional support for H2F test events and exercises are located on the Army Combat Fitness Test website at https://www.army.mil/acft/.

1. POWER JUMP

5-3. The Power Jump is the first exercise in Conditioning Drill 1. This exercise reinforces correct jumping and landing skill, requires good balance and coordination, and develops explosive strength to move off the ground. Figure 5-1 on page 5-2 breaks down the movement Soldiers conduct at a moderate cadence:

- The starting position for the Power Jump is the Straddle Stance position with hands on hips.
- On count 1, squat with the heels flat while rounding spine forward and reaching to the ground. Place palms on the ground. Gaze remains forward.
- On count 2, jump forcefully from the ground, swinging the arms up and overhead to unweight the body and increase the height of the jump. Palms face inward.
- On count 3, return to the count 1 position after landing softly with feet directed forward and shoulder-width apart.
- On count 4, return to the starting position.

Figure 5-1. CD1.1 Power Jump

2. V-UP

5-4.   The V-Up is the second exercise in Conditioning Drill 1. This exercise develops the abdominal and hip flexor muscles for more vigorous training and combat tasks such as the leg tuck, rope traverse, and surmounting obstacles. Figure 5-2 breaks down the movement Soldier conduct at a moderate cadence:

- The starting position for the V-Up is the Supine position with arms on the ground at 45 degrees from the body, knees bent to 90 degrees. The head is 1–2 inches off the ground.
- On count 1, raise the legs and trunk at the same time into a V position, using the arms to balance. Keep the knees straight and the head aligned with the trunk—neither bent forward nor extended backwards.
- On count 2, return under control to the starting position. Avoid dropping the legs.
- On count 3, repeat count 1.
- On count 4, return to the count 2 position.

Figure 5-2. CD1.2 V-Up

3. MOUNTAIN CLIMBER

5-5.   The Mountain Climber is the third exercise in Conditioning Drill 1. This exercise develops the ability to quickly power out of the Front Leaning Rest position into a Run or a Crouch Run. Figure 5-3 breaks down the movement Soldiers conduct at a moderate cadence:

- The starting position for the Mountain Climber is the Front Leaning Rest with the left foot below the chest and the left knee between the arms.
- On count 1, shift body weight to the hands while changing the position of the feet. Keep the back straight and keep the hips from moving up and down throughout the exercise.
- On count 2, reverse the movement performed in count 1 to return to the starting position.
- On count 3, repeat count 1.
- On count 4, return to the starting position.

Figure 5-3. CD1.3 Mountain Climber

4. LEG-TUCK AND TWIST

5-6.   The Leg-Tuck and Twist is the fourth exercise in Conditioning Drill 1. This exercise strengthens the trunk and hip muscle coordination while promoting control of trunk rotation. It is an advanced body weight exercise that prepares for more vigorous training, testing, and combat tasks. Figure 5-4 breaks down the movement Soldiers conduct at a moderate cadence:

- The starting position for the Leg-Tuck and Twist is the supported reclining Sitting position. Hands are on the ground to the rear of the shoulders, palms down. Legs are straight and kept together with the feet 8–12 inches above the ground.
- On count 1, raise the legs while rotating onto the left buttock and drawing the knees toward the left shoulder. Maintain control of the leg movement and trunk position.
- On count 2, reverse the movement performed in count 1 to return to the starting position.
- On count 3, repeat count 1, this time rotating the legs to the right.
- On count 4, return to the starting position.

Figure 5-4. CD1.4 Leg-Tuck and Twist

5. SINGLE-LEG PUSH-UP

5-7.   The Single-Leg Push-Up is the final exercise in Conditioning Drill 1. This exercise strengthens the muscles of the chest and hips as well as increases the challenge to shoulder stability. When conducted to standard, it safely prepares Soldiers for more vigorous pushing motions required in training, testing, and combat tasks. Figure 5-5 breaks down the movement Soldiers conduct at a moderate cadence:

- The starting position for the Single-Leg Push-Up is the Front Leaning Rest. Hands are directly beneath the shoulders with fingers spread. Feet are together. The body forms a straight line from the top of the head to the heels.
- On count 1, bend the elbows, lowering the body until the upper arms are parallel to the ground. At the same time, raise the left leg until the toe is level or just above the right heel. Keep the left knee straight. This is not a high leg raise or hyper-extension of the hip.

- On count 2, reverse the movement performed in count 1 to return to the starting position.
- On count 3, repeat count 1, moving the right leg the same way that the left leg moved in count 1.
- On count 4, return to the starting position.

Figure 5-5. CD1.5 Single-Leg Push-up

CONDITIONING DRILL 1 (MODIFIED) (CD1 MOD)

5-8. Conditioning Drill 1 (Modified) (known as CD1 MOD) consists of five exercises designed to improve muscular strength and endurance, balance and coordination for Soldiers with limited range of motion. The modified Conditioning Drill 1 is ideal for those Soldiers undergoing rehabilitation from injury by limiting muscle strain and flexion of the arms, shoulders, legs, and core muscles. Modified Conditioning Drill 1 exercises consists of the following exercises: Power Jump (modified), V-Up (modified), Mountain Climber (modified), Leg-Tuck and Twist (modified), and Single-Leg Push-Up (modified).

1. POWER JUMP (MODIFIED)

5-9. The modified Power Jump replaces the first exercise in Conditioning Drill 1. This modification decreases the range of motion and limits the use of the arms and legs, and eliminates impact on the legs. Figure 5-6 on page 5-6 breaks down the movement Soldiers conduct at a moderate cadence:

- The starting position for the modified Power Jump is the Straddle Stance position with hands on hips.
- On count 1, squat with the heels flat, keeping the spine straight while reaching to the ground. Face the palms toward the ground. Gaze remains forward.
- On count 2, reach quickly up and overhead, raising off both heels without the feet leaving the ground. Palms face inward.
- On count 3, return to the count 1 position.
- On count 4, return to the starting position.

Figure 5-6. CD1 MOD1 Power Jump (modified)

2. V-UP (MODIFIED)

5-10. The modified V-Up replaces the second exercise in Conditioning Drill 1. This modification decreases the range of motion and limits the use of the arm, leg, and core muscles. Figure 5-7 breaks down the movement Soldiers conduct at a moderate cadence:

- The starting position for the modified V-Up is the Supine position with arms on the ground at 45 degrees from the body, knees bent to 90 degrees, feet flat on the ground. The head may be on the ground or 1–2 inches off the ground.
- On count 1, bend the knees, raising the legs and trunk at the same time, using the arms to balance. Keep the head aligned with the trunk—neither bent forward nor extended backwards. Bring the knees toward the chest.
- On count 2, return under control to the starting position, placing the feet flat on the ground with knees bent. Avoid dropping the legs.
- On count 4, return to the count 2 position.

Figure 5-7. CD1 MOD2 V-Up (modified)

5-11. Other potential modifications include the following:
- Starting position in Supine position with knees bent:
  - On count 1, the trunk moves up.
  - On count 2, the left leg lifts from the ground.
  - On count 3, the left leg returns to the ground.
  - On count 4, the trunk returns to the ground.
- Starting position is with the trunk in the Sitting position, supported by the arms:
  - On count 1, left knee moves to the chest.
  - On count 2, left knee returns to starting position.
  - On count 3, right knee moves to the chest.
  - On count 4, right knee returns to the starting position.
- Starting position is Supine position with knees bent:
  - On count 1, left knee moves to the chest.
  - On count 2, left knee returns to starting position.
  - On count 3, right knee moves to the chest.
  - On count 4, right knee returns to the starting position.

3. MOUNTAIN CLIMBER (MODIFIED)

5-12. The Mountain Climber (modified) replaces the third exercise in Conditioning Drill 1. This modification decreases the range of motion and limits the use of the arm, leg, and core muscles. Figure 5-8 breaks down the movement Soldiers conduct at a moderate cadence:
- The starting position for the modified Mountain Climber is the Front Leaning Rest with the left foot next to the right knee and the left knee under the Soldier's hips.
- On count 1, shift body weight to the hands while changing the position of the feet. Keep the back straight and keep the hips from moving up and down throughout the exercise.
- On count 2, reverse the movement performed in count 1 to return to the starting position.
- On count 3, repeat count 1.
- On count 4, return to the starting position.

Figure 5-8. CD1 MOD3 Mountain Climber (modified)

5-13. Other potential modifications for Mountain Climber include the following:
- Starting position as in paragraph 5-12:
  - On count 1, one leg moves toward the chest.
  - On count 2, the same leg returns to the starting position.
  - On count 3, repeat count 1.
  - On count 4, repeat count 2.
- Starting position is the Straddle Stance position:

- On count 1, left knee moves to the chest as the Soldier balances on the right leg.
- On count 2, left leg returns to starting position.
- On count 3, right knee moves to the chest as the Soldier balances on the left leg.
- On count 4, right leg returns to the starting position.
- Starting position is the Supine position with knees bent:
  - On count 1, left knee moves to the chest.
  - On count 2, left knee returns to starting position.
  - On count 3, right knee moves to the chest.
  - On count 4, right knee returns to the starting position.

4. LEG-TUCK AND TWIST (MODIFIED)

5-14. The Leg-Tuck and Twist (modified) replaces the fourth exercise in Conditioning Drill 1. This modification decreases the range of motion and limits the use of the arm, leg, and core muscles. Figure 5-9 breaks down the movement Soldiers conduct at a moderate cadence:

- The starting position for the modified Leg-Tuck and Twist is the supported reclining Sitting position. Hands are on the ground to the rear of the shoulders, palms down. Legs are bent with feet flat on the ground.
- On count 1, raise the legs while rotating onto the left buttock and drawing the knees toward the left shoulder. Maintain control of the bent knee and trunk position.
- On count 2, reverse the movement performed in count 1 to return to the starting position.
- On count 3, repeat count 1, this time rotating the legs to the right.
- On count 4, return to the starting position.

Figure 5-9. CD1 MOD4 Leg-Tuck and Twist (modified)

5-15. Other modifications include the following:

- Starting position as above, alternate single leg movement.
- Starting position is the Supine position with the knees bent, and trunk, arms, and head on the ground:
  - On count 1, left knee moves to the chest.
  - On count 2, left knee returns to starting position.
  - On count 3, right knee moves to the chest.
  - On count 4, right knee returns to the starting position.
- Starting position is the Supine position with knees bent to 45 degrees:
  - On count 1, both knees lift up and to the left.
  - On count 2, return to the starting position.
  - On count 3, both knees lift up to the right.
  - On count 4, return to the starting position.

5. SINGLE-LEG PUSH-UP (MODIFIED)

5-16. The Single-Leg Push-Up (Modified) replaces the final exercise in Conditioning Drill 1. This modified exercise limits the range of motion and weight on the ankles, shoulders, arms, and wrists. Figure 5-10 breaks down the movement Soldiers conduct at a moderate cadence:

- Modify the movement into the starting position—avoid Squat and rear thrust of the legs.
- The starting position for the modified Single Leg Push-Up is the Six-Point Stance position. Hands are directly beneath the shoulders with fingers spread. The body forms a straight line from the head to the knees. Feet point to the rear.
- On count 1, bend the elbows, lowering the body until the upper arms are parallel to the ground.
- On count 2, return to the starting position. If necessary, reduce the range of motion of the elbow to accommodate for the injury.
- On count 3, repeat count 1, reducing the range of motion if necessary.
- On count 4, return to the starting position.

Figure 5-10. CD1 MOD5 Push-Up (modified)

5-17. Other modifications include—

- Sustained Front Leaning Rest for time.
- Sustained Front Leaning Rest on elbows for time.

CONDITIONING DRILL 2 (CD2)

5-18. Conditioning Drill 2 (known as CD2) consists of five exercises designed to develop and improve strength, agility, and mobility. The Conditioning Drill 2 consists of the following exercises: Turn and Lunge, Supine Bicycle, Half Jack, Swimmer, and 8-Count T Push-Up.

1. TURN AND LUNGE

5-19. The Turn and Lunge is the first exercise in Conditioning Drill 2. This exercise develops the agility needed to rotate, lower, and raise the body for effective changes of direction. Figure 5-11 on page 5-10 breaks down the movement when conducted in a formation at a slow cadence:

- The starting position for the Turn and Lunge is the Straddle Stance position with hands on hips.
- On count 1, turn 90 degrees to the left pivoting on the right foot while stepping with the left. Perform a Forward Lunge facing left reaching to the ground with the right hand between the legs. The left arm moves rearward at the left side of the body. Keep the head in line with the spine.
- On count 2, stand up, rotate to the right to return to the starting position, stepping with the right foot and pivoting on the ball of the left foot.
- On count 3, repeat count 1 to the right, stepping with the right foot, pivoting on the left.
- On count 4, rotate to the left, pivoting on the right foot and stepping with the left to return to the starting position.
- Complete 5–10 repetitions, continuing to pivot on the rear foot and step with the lead foot.

Figure 5-11. CD2.1 Turn and Lunge

2. SUPINE BICYCLE

5-20. The Supine Bicycle is the second exercise in Conditioning Drill 2. This exercise strengthens the muscles of the abdomen and controls the rotation of the trunk. Hand placement and controlled movement make this a safe way to develop strength and endurance for more vigorous training, testing, and combat tasks. Figure 5-12 breaks down the movement when conducted in a formation at a slow cadence:

- The starting position for the Supine Bicycle is the Supine position with hands resting on top of the head—not the back of the head—and knees and hips bent to 90 degrees. The head will be 2–4 inches off the ground.
- On count 1, bring the left knee toward the chest while flexing and rotating the trunk to the left. Attempt to touch the right elbow with the right thigh. At the same time, extend the right knee to straighten the right leg.
- On count 2, return under control to the starting position. There is a pause in this movement on count 2—it is not a continuous movement to the opposite side.
- On count 3, repeat count 1 to the opposite side.
- On count 4, return to the starting position.
- Complete 5–10 repetitions.

Figure 5-12. CD2.2 Supine Bicycle

3. HALF JACK

5-21. The Half Jack is the third exercise in Conditioning Drill 2. The purpose of this exercise is to jump and land with the legs apart, controlling the landing while moving the feet laterally. Movement of the arms in the frontal (dividing the front and back) plane to a point parallel to the ground avoids the potential for shoulder impingement caused when the arms repeatedly move higher than shoulder height. Figure 5-13 breaks down the movement when conducted in a formation at a moderate cadence:

- The starting position for the Half Jack is the Position of Attention.
- On count 1, jump and land with the feet shoulder-width apart and pointed straight ahead. The arms are straight out to the side of the body, palms down with fingers and thumbs extended and joined. The arms will not move beyond the point where they are parallel to the ground.
- On count 2, reverse the movement performed in count 1 to return to the starting position.
- On count 3, repeat count 1.
- On count 4, return to the starting position.
- Complete 5–10 repetitions.

Figure 5-13. CD2.3 Half Jack

4. SWIMMER

5-22. The Swimmer is the fourth exercise in Conditioning Drill 2. This exercise strengthens the back of the shoulder, neck, spine, hips, and legs—often referred to as the posterior chain of muscles. These muscles are used in training and combat tasks such as low crawling, prone firing, and swimming. Figure 5-14 breaks down the movement Soldiers conduct at a slow cadence:

- The starting position for the Swimmer is the Prone position with the arms extended overhead, palms down and on the ground. Toes are pointed to the rear.
- On count 1, raise the left arm and right leg off the ground while lifting the head up and arching the back slightly. Gaze should be "down-range" or parallel to the ground at this point.
- On count 2, reverse the movement performed in count 1 to return to the starting position.
- On count 3, repeat count 1, this time with the opposite arm and leg.
- On count 4, return to the starting position.
- Complete 5–10 repetitions.

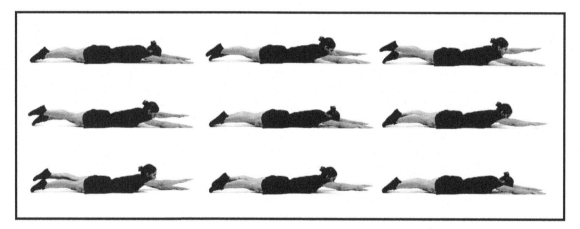

Figure 5-14. CD2.4 Swimmer

5. 8-COUNT T PUSH-UP

5-23. The 8-Count T Push-Up is the final exercise in Conditioning Drill 2. This exercise develops total body strength, endurance, and mobility. Releasing the hands from the ground, in addition to moving the arms to the T position, emphasizes full push and reach motions. Figure 5-15 breaks down the movement as Soldiers in formation conduct it at a moderate cadence:

- The starting position for the 8-Count T Push-Up is the Position of Attention.
- On count 1, assume the Squat position.
- On count 2, thrust the legs backwards in to the Front Leaning Rest Position.
- On count 3, bend the elbows lowering the body to the ground.
- On count 4, release the hands from the ground, moving the arms directly out to the side into the T position—the same position used in the T-Raise exercise. Hands may be on or off the ground in the T position.
- On count 6, perform a push up from the ground into the Front Leaning Rest position. Keep the body in a straight line from the head to the bottom of the heels.
- On count 7, return to the Squat position.
- On count 8, return to the Position of Attention.
- Complete 5–10 repetitions.

Figure 5-15. CD2.5 8-Count T-Push-Up

CONDITIONING DRILL 3 (CD3)

5-24. Conditioning Drill 3 is an advanced plyometric drill. Repeated jumping, landing, and changing body positions place greater demands on the lower extremities than in Conditioning Drills 1 and 2. Soldiers progress to Conditioning Drill 3 after mastering the movements and being able to tolerate 10 repetitions of Conditioning Drills 1 and 2. Progression to Conditioning Drill 3 should include precise instruction and practice of each exercise. For most Soldiers, 10 repetitions of the final exercise in Conditioning Drill 3, the Alternate Staggered Squat Jump, will be a culminating moment in the physical training week.

1. Y SQUAT

5-25. The Y Squat is the first exercise in Conditioning Drill 3. This exercise combines upper and lower body squatting strength, mobility, and endurance. Figure 5-16 on page 5-14 breaks down the exercise as Soldiers conduct it a formation at slow cadence:

- The starting position for the Y Squat is the Straddle Stance position with feet slightly wider than shoulder width, arms overhead in the Y position, and shoulders pulled back.
- On count 1, lower the body as far as possible without rounding the back, keeping the shoulders drawn rearward, arms forming a Y overhead. Heels remain on the ground throughout the movement.
- On count 2, return to the starting position.
- On count 3, repeat count 1.
- On count 4, repeat count 2.
- Build up to 10 repetitions. After the final repetition, return to turn to the starting position.

Figure 5-16. CD3.1 Y Squat

2. SINGLE-LEG DEADLIFT

5-26. The Single-Leg Deadlift is the second exercise in Conditioning Drill 3. This exercise develops strength and flexibility of the lower back and lower extremities. Figure 5-17 breaks down the exercise as Soldiers conduct it in a formation at slow cadence:

- The starting position for the Single-Leg Deadlift is the Straddle Stance position with hands on hips.
- On count 1, maintain balance on the left leg while bending forward at the waist. Reach straight down toward the ground while raising the right leg up to the rear.
- On count 2, reverse the movement to return to the starting position.
- On count 3, repeat count 1 balancing on the right leg.
- On count 4, repeat count 2 to return to the starting position.
- The hands may touch the ground with fingers spread to assist with balance at the end of counts 1 and 3.
- Build up to 10 correctly performed repetitions.

Figure 5-17. CD3.2 Single-Leg Deadlift

3. SIDE-TO-SIDE KNEE LIFTS

5-27. The Side-to-Side Knee Lifts is the third exercise in Conditioning Drill 3. This exercise combines upper and lower body strength, mobility, and endurance. It is a dynamic test of single leg balance and total body coordination. Figure 5-18 on page 5-16 breaks down the exercise as Soldiers conduct it in a formation at moderate cadence:

- The starting position for the Side-to-Side Knee Lifts is the Straddle Stance position with hands on hips.
- On count 1, hop to the left foot while simultaneously drawing the right knee toward the chest. The right hand moves comfortably down toward the right ankle. The left hand touches the right knee.
- On count 2, hop to the right foot while simultaneously drawing the left knee toward the chest. The left hand moves comfortably down to the side toward the left ankle and the right hand touches the left knee.
- On count 3, repeat count 1.
- On count 4, repeat count 2.
- Keep the head up and the back straight throughout the movement. Try not to lean forward.
- Build up to 10 correctly performed repetitions.

Figure 5-18. CD3.3 Side-to-Side Knee Lifts

4. FRONT KICK ALTERNATE TOE TOUCH

5-28. The Front Kick Alternate Toe Touch is the fourth exercise in Conditioning Drill 3. This exercise develops balance, coordination, and flexibility of the legs and trunk. Figure 5-19 breaks down the exercise as Soldiers conduct it in a formation at moderate cadence:

- The starting position for the Front Kick Alternate Toe Touch is the Straddle Stance position with hands on hips.
- On count 1, raise the left leg to the front of the body until it is parallel to the ground while simultaneously bending forward at the waist, extending the right arm forward and reaching with the right hand toward the left foot. The left arm reaches rearward.
- On count 2, return to the starting position.
- On count 3, raise the right leg to the front of the body until it is parallel to the ground while simultaneously bending forward at the waist, extending the left arm forward and reaching with the left hand toward the right foot. The right arm reaches rearward.
- On count 4, return to the starting position.
- Build up to 10 correctly performed repetitions.

Figure 5-19. CD3.4 Front Kick Alternate Toe Touch

5. TUCK JUMP

5-29. The Tuck Jump is the fifth exercise in Conditioning Drill 3. This exercise develops explosive strength in the legs. Figure 5-20 on page 5-18 shows the exercise as Soldiers conduct it in formation at slow cadence:

- The starting position for the Tuck Jump is the Straddle Stance position with arms at the sides.
- On count 1, perform a half squat while driving the arms rearward. Jump up from this position pulling both feet under the hips and tucking the knees to the chest. Wrap the arms around the front of the knees before landing softly on the balls of the feet.
- On count 2, stand up into the starting position.
- On count 3, repeat count 1.
- On count 4, repeat count 2.
- The cadence is slow to allow proper preparation for and recovery from the explosive jumps on counts 1 and 3.
- Build up to 10 correctly performed repetitions.

Figure 5-20. CD3.5 Tuck Jump

6. STRADDLE RUN FORWARD AND BACKWARD

5-30. The Straddle Run Forward and Backward is the sixth exercise in Conditioning Drill 3. This exercise combines upper body and lower body plyometric skill, coordination, and anaerobic endurance. Figure 5-21 breaks down the exercise as Soldiers conduct it in a formation at moderate cadence;

- The starting position for the Straddle Run Forward and Backward is the Straddle Stance position.
- On count 1, bound forward to the left with the left leg, swinging the right arm forward and to the left and the left arm rearward.
- On count 2, bound forward to the right with the right leg, swinging the left arm forward and to the right and the right arm rearward.
- On count 3, repeat count 1.
- On count 4, repeat count 2.
- On count 5, bound backward and to the left with the left leg, swinging the left arm forward and right arm rearward.
- On count 6, bound backward and to the right with the right leg, swinging the right arm forward and the left arm rearward.
- On count 7, repeat count 5.
- On count 8, repeat count 6.
- Repeat this exercise 5–10 times.
- After the final count, return to the starting position.

Figure 5-21. CD3.6 Straddle Run Forward and Backward

7. HALF-SQUAT LATERALS

5-31. Half-Squat Laterals is the seventh exercise in Conditioning Drill 3. This exercise combines upper body and lower body plyometric skill and anaerobic endurance. Figure 5-22 on page 5-20 breaks down the exercise as Soldiers conduct it in a formation at moderate cadence:

- The starting position for Half-Squat Laterals is the Straddle Stance position, slightly crouched in a half squat with hands facing forward at chest height. Feet will be directed straight ahead throughout the exercise.
- On count 1, maintaining the trunk in a forward orientation, make a half-squat step-hop to the left.
- On count 2, maintaining the same trunk orientation, make a half-squat step-hop to the right.
- On count 3, maintaining the trunk in the same orientation, make another half-squat step-hop to the right.
- On count 4, maintaining the trunk in the same orientation, make a half-squat step-hop to the left to return to the starting position.
- Repeat this exercise 5–10 times.

Figure 5-22. CD3.7 Half-Squat Laterals

8. FROG JUMPS FORWARD AND BACKWARD

5-32. The Frog Jumps Forward and Backward is the eighth exercise in Conditioning Drill 3. This exercise combines upper body and lower body plyometric skill and anaerobic endurance. Figure 5-23 breaks down the exercise as Soldiers conduct it in a formation at moderate cadence:

- The starting position for the Frog Jumps Forward and Backward is the Straddle Stance, slightly crouched in a half squat with hands facing forward at chest height. Feet will be directed straight ahead throughout the exercise.
- On count 1, maintaining the trunk in a forward orientation, make a half-squat hop forward.
- On count 2, maintaining the same trunk orientation, make a half-squat hop backward.
- On count 3, maintaining the trunk in the same orientation, make another half-squat hop backward.
- On count 4, maintaining the trunk in the same orientation, make a half-squat hop forward to return to the starting position.
- Repeat this exercise 5–10 times.

Figure 5-23. CD3.8 Frog Jumps Forward and Backward

9. ALTERNATE ¼-TURN JUMP

5-33. The Alternate ¼-Turn Jump is the ninth exercise in Conditioning Drill 3. This exercise combines upper body and lower body plyometric skill with trunk control and anaerobic endurance. Figure 5-24 on page 5-22 breaks down the exercise as Soldiers conduct it in a formation at moderate cadence:

- The starting position for the Alternate ¼-Turn Jump is the Straddle Stance position, slightly crouched in a half squat with hands facing forward at chest height.
- On count 1, jump upwards and twist the hips to turn the legs 90 degrees to the left. The Soldier will resist trunk rotation, maintaining a forward head and chest orientation for all counts. Do not cross the legs or allow the feet to become staggered.
- On count 2, return to the starting position with feet the same width apart as in the starting position.
- On count 3, jump upwards and twist the hips to turn the legs 90 degrees to the right.
- On count 4, return to the starting position.
- After the final repetition, return to the starting position.

Figure 5-24. CD3.9 Alternate ¼-Turn Jump

10. ALTERNATE STAGGERED SQUAT JUMP

5-34. The Alternate Staggered Squat Jump is the final exercise in Conditioning Drill 3. Occurring at the end of Conditioning Drill 3, and therefore at the end of most physical training sessions, this exercise requires advanced levels of movement skill and anaerobic endurance. Ten repetitions of this exercise, following on from its predecessor Conditioning Drill 3 exercises truly tests a Soldier's grit. Figure 5-25 breaks down the exercise as Soldiers conduct it in a formation at slow cadence:

- The starting position for the Alternate Staggered Squat Jump is the Straddle Stance position with staggered legs with left leg back and arms at sides. The trunk is flexed slightly forward.
- On count 1, squat and touch the ground between the legs with the fingertips of the left hand. Jump forcefully into the air, switching legs in mid-air to land with the right leg back and arms at the sides.
- On count 2, squat and touch the ground between the legs with the fingertips of the right hand. Jump forcefully into the air, switching legs in mid-air to land with the left leg back and arms at the sides.
- On count 3, repeat count 1.
- On count 4, repeat count 2.
- After the final repetition, return to turn to the starting position.

Figure 5-25. CD3.10 Alternate Staggered Squat Jump

This page intentionally left blank.

Chapter 6

Climbing and Guerilla Drills

CLIMBING DRILL 1 (CL1)

6-1. Climbing Drills (known as (CL) provide a broad variety of pulling exercises to improve upper body strength and endurance. This range of exercises allows Soldiers to pull up as well as onto and over obstacles. These drills also involve spotters whose skill and strength will play an important role in the safety and success of the Soldier in training, testing, and combat situations. Spotters assist when exercisers cannot perform 5 repetitions of all exercises unassisted. Spotters provide the least amount of assistance possible to ensure that the exercise is completed safely and through the greatest range of motion. Too much assistance from a spotter may lead to an inadequate improvement in performance by the exercising Soldier.

6-2. Videos of Climbing and Guerilla Drills on the Central Army Registry website at https://atiam.train.army.mil/catalog/search?current=true&filetype=mp4&respect_date=5%2F1%2F2020&search_terms=CIMT demonstrate movements. (Copy and paste this address after accessing the Central Army Registry website if the demonstrations do not populate.) Additional support for H2F test events and exercises are located on the Army Combat Fitness Test website at https://www.army.mil/acft/.

1. STRAIGHT-ARM PULL

6-3. The Straight-Arm Pull is the first exercise in Climbing Drill 1. This exercise develops the Soldier's ability to initiate the pull-up motion, maintain grip, and contract upper back and shoulder muscles. Figure 6-1 on page 6-2 breaks down the exercise as Soldiers conduct it with two spotters:

- The starting position for the Straight-Arm Pull is the Straight-Arm Hang using the closed overhand grip.
- If the Soldier states "No spotter needed," the two spotters are not required. Otherwise, the spotters assume the Straddle Stance position with staggered legs in front and behind the exerciser.
- The front spotter places palms toward the exerciser at chest height to support the exerciser if his or her grip fails.
- The rear spotter places palms toward the exerciser at chest height to support the exerciser if his or her grip fails. The rear spotter assists in guiding the exerciser to the foot pegs on the climbing bar.
- On the command, "UP," move from the starting position, keep the arms straight, and pull the body up with the effect of raising the head between the arms. The chest will move up toward the bar and the shoulder blades will move together.
- On the command, "DOWN," return to the starting position.
- Repeat the exercise 5–10 times.

Figure 6-1. CL1.1 Straight Arm Pull

2. HEEL HOOK

6-4. The Heel Hook is the second exercise in Climbing Drills 1 and 2. This exercise develops the Soldier's ability to pull up and hook the legs onto a ledge, rope, or rail. Figure 6-2 breaks down the exercise as Soldiers conduct it with two spotters to assist:

- The starting position for the Heel Hook is the Straight-Arm Hang using the closed overhand grip.
- If the Soldier states, "No spotter needed," the two spotters are not required. Otherwise, the spotters assume the Straddle Stance position with staggered legs on either side of the exerciser.
- Each spotter prepares to assist by positioning one hand behind and off the back of the knee and the low back. They will be prepared at all times to assist in the movement and catch the exerciser if his or her grip fails.
- On the command, "UP," flex the elbows, knees, and hips to raise both feet above the bar, crossing one ankle over the other.
- On the command, "DOWN," return to the starting position.
- The spotters may assist in guiding the exerciser to the foot pegs after the command "DOWN" prior to the command "DISMOUNT."

Figure 6-2. CL1.2 Heel Hook

3. PULL-UP

6-5.   The Pull-Up is the third exercise in Climbing Drills 1 and 2. This exercise develops the Soldier's ability to pull up without using the legs. Figure 6-3 on page 6-4 breaks down the exercise as Soldiers conduct it with two spotters to assist:

- The starting position for the Pull-Up is the Straight-Arm Hang using the closed overhand grip.
- If the Soldier states, "No spotter needed," the two spotters are not required. Otherwise, the spotters assume the Straddle Stance position with staggered legs in the front and back of the exerciser.
- The front spotter places palms toward the exerciser at chest height to support the exerciser if his or her grip fails.
- The rear spotter holds the exerciser's feet against his or her thighs or abdomen to support the movement up. Once the Soldier is up, the rear spotter stops assisting.
- On the command, "UP," flex the elbows, raising the body in a straight line until the head is above the bar.
- On the command, "DOWN," return to the starting position.
- Repeat the exercise 5–10 times.
- The spotters may assist in guiding the exerciser to the foot pegs after the command "DOWN" prior to the command "DISMOUNT."

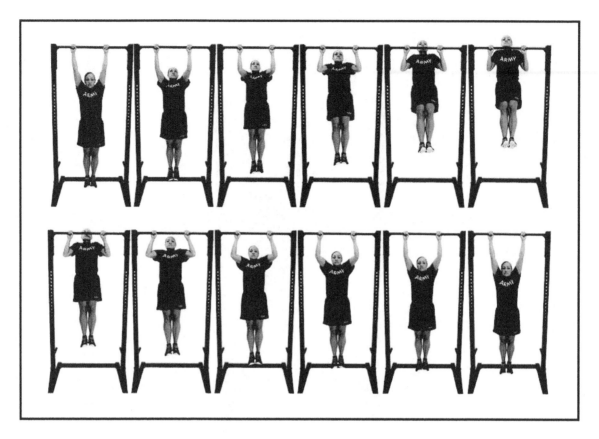

Figure 6-3. CL1.3 Pull-Up

4. LEG TUCK

6-6.   The Leg Tuck is the fourth exercise in Climbing Drills 1 and 2. This exercise combines upper body and abdominal strength to develop the Soldier's ability to hang while moving the legs into different support positions for climbing. Figure 6-4 breaks down the exercise as Soldiers conduct it with two spotters to assist:

- The starting position for the Leg Tuck is the Straight-Arm Hang using the closed alternating overhand grip.
- If the Soldier states, "No spotter needed," the two spotters are not required. Otherwise, the spotters assume Straddle Stance positions on either side of the exerciser.
- Each spotter prepares to assist by positioning one hand behind and off the back of the knee and the low back. He or she will be prepared at all times to assist in the movement and catch the exerciser if his or her grip fails.
- On the command, "UP," flex the elbows and hips raising the legs until the thighs touch the elbows.
- On the command, "DOWN," return to the starting position.
- Repeat the exercise 5–10 times.
- The spotters may assist in guiding the exerciser to the foot pegs after the command "DOWN" prior to the command "DISMOUNT."

Figure 6-4. CL1.4 Leg Tuck

5. ALTERNATING GRIP PULL-UP

6-7.   The Alternating Grip Pull-Up is the final exercise in Climbing Drills 1 and 2. This exercise develops the Soldier's ability to pull up and hook the legs onto a ledge, rope, or rail. Figure 6-5 on page 6-6 breaks down the exercise as Soldiers conduct it with two spotters to assist:

- The starting position for the Alternating Grip Pull-Up is the Straight-Arm Hang using the closed alternating grip. This positions the Soldier perpendicular to the bar.
- If the Soldier states, "No spotter needed," the two spotters are not required. Otherwise, the spotters assume the Straddle Stance position with staggered legs in the front and back of the exerciser.
- The front spotter places palms toward the exerciser at chest height to support the exerciser if his or her grip fails.
- The rear spotter holds the exerciser's feet against his or her thighs or abdomen to support the movement up. Once the Soldier is up, the rear spotter stops assisting.
- On count 1, flex the elbows, raising the body up so that the head moves to the side of the bar.
- On count 2, return to the starting position.
- Repeat the exercise 5–10 times.
- The spotters may assist in guiding the exerciser to the foot pegs after the command "DOWN" prior to the command "DISMOUNT."

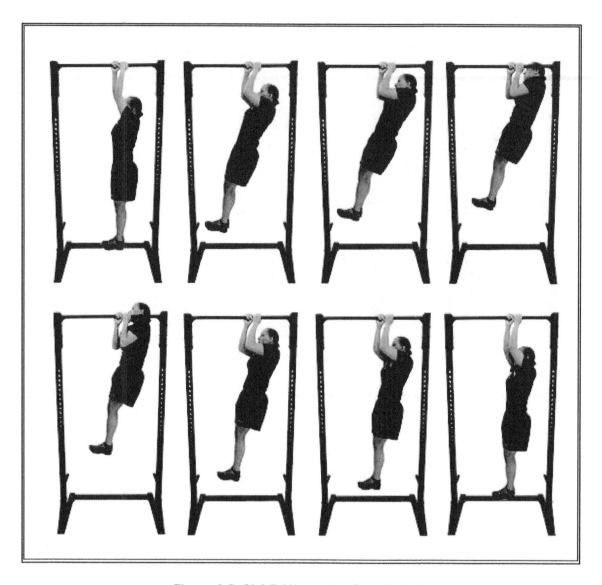

Figure 6-5. CL1.5 Alternating Grip Pull-Up

CLIMBING DRILL 2 (CL2)

6-8.   Climbing Drill 2 is a higher intensity drill than Climbing Drill 1. Soldiers conduct Climbing Drill 2 in the Sustaining Phase to prepare Soldiers for critical tasks under a fighting load such as climbing, traversing a rope, and pulling the body up on a ledge or through a window. Soldiers increase resistance by performing Climbing Drill 2 wearing the Army combat uniform (known as ACU), load bearing equipment or load bearing vest, improved outer tactical vest, and advanced combat helmet, and carrying an individual weapon. Due to the heavier load placed on the exercising Soldiers, spotters need to be ready to assist much earlier in Climbing Drill 2. The goal is to perform 5–10 repetitions of all five exercises unassisted. Except for the first exercise, Flexed-Arm Hang, the five exercises of Climbing Drill 2 are the same as Climbing Drill 1.

1. FLEXED-ARM HANG

6-9.   The Flexed-Arm Hang is the first exercise in Climbing Drill 2. This exercise develops the Soldier's upper body muscular endurance, enabling him or her to sustain the Up position. Figure 6-6 breaks down the exercise as Soldiers conduct it with two spotters to assist:

- The starting position for the Flexed Arm Hang is the Straight-Arm Hang using the closed overhand grip.
- If the Soldier states, "No spotter needed," the two spotters are not required. Otherwise, the spotters assume the Straddle Stance position with staggered legs in the front and back of the exerciser.
- The front spotter places palms toward the exerciser at chest height to support the exerciser if his or her grip fails.
- The rear spotter holds the exerciser's feet against his or her thighs or abdomen to support the movement up. Once the Soldier is up, the rear spotter stops assisting.
- On the command, "UP," flex the elbows to pull up, raising the head above the bar. Hold this position for a count of 5 seconds.
- On the command, "DOWN," return to the starting position.
- If the Soldier cannot hold the up position for 5 seconds, he or she will return to the starting position.
- A longer duration hold is appropriate in Soldiers who can perform all the Climbing Drill exercises for 5 repetitions to standard without assist.
- The spotters may assist in guiding the exerciser to the foot pegs after the command "DOWN" prior to the command "DISMOUNT."

Figure 6-6. CL2.1 Flexed-Arm Hang

2. HEEL HOOK

6-10. This Heel Hook drill is the same as Climbing Drill 1. See paragraph 6-4.

3. PULL-UP

6-11. This Pull-Up is the same as Climbing Drill 1. See paragraph 6-5.

4. LEG TUCK

6-12. This Leg Tuck is the same as Climbing Drill 1. See paragraph 6-6.

5. ALTERNATING GRIP PULL-UP

6-13. This Alternating Grip Pull-Up is the same as Climbing Drill 1. See paragraph 6-7.

GUERILLA DRILL (GD)

6-14. In the Sustaining Phase, the Guerilla Drill provides an advanced method of developing leg power, coordination, and the ability to lift and carry another Soldier. The three exercises in the Guerilla Drill are always performed in order, at quick time, and with careful attention to precise movement skill. When Soldiers can precisely execute the drill across the 25-meter course, they can progress up to three sets of the drill.

1. SHOULDER ROLL

6-15. The Shoulder Roll is the first exercise in Guerilla Drill. This exercise develops the Soldier's ability to safely fall and roll up to a standing position. Figure 6-7 breaks down the exercise as Soldiers would conduct it in a formation:

- The starting position for the Shoulder Roll is the Straddle Stance position.
- From the starting position, step forward with the left foot, squat down, and make a wheel with the arms by placing the left hand on the ground with the fingers facing to the rear. Point the lead elbow in the direction of the desired travel.
- The right hand is also on the ground with the fingers facing forward. Tuck the chin to avoid injury to the neck.
- Push off with the right leg and roll over the left shoulder along the left side of the body. Do not roll onto the neck. The push must generate enough momentum to bring the Soldier up the knees.
- Continue to the feet by pushing off with the rear leg to stand up.
- To roll to the opposite side, step forward, and switch hand and leg positions.
- Continue alternating shoulder rolls until across the 25-meter line.

Figure 6-7. GD1 Shoulder Roll

2. LUNGE WALK

6-16. The Lunge Walk is the second exercise in the Guerilla Drill. This exercise develops the leg power needed to move under control in a crouch. This strength improves other movements to and from the ground. Figure 6-8 breaks down the exercise as Soldiers conduct it in a formation:

- From the starting position, the Position of Attention, step forward with the left foot, stepping as in a Lunge and swinging the opposite arm until the upper arm is parallel to the ground.
- Lightly touch the knee of the rear leg to the ground with each step.
- Step forward and under the body with the right leg, avoiding raising the trunk. Avoid swinging the leg out to the side to clear the ground.
- Continue alternating leg and arm movements until crossing the 25-meter line.

Figure 6-8. GD2 Lunge Walk

3. SOLDIER CARRY

6-17. The Soldier Carry is the third exercise in the Guerilla Drill. This exercise develops the Soldier's ability to safely carry a conscious or unconscious Soldier of comparable size. Soldier A is the Soldier performing the carry. Soldier B is the Soldier being carried. Figure 6-9 on page 6-10 breaks down the exercise as Soldiers conduct it in a formation:

- In the starting position, Soldier B is in the Prone position with arms overhead. Soldier A is in the Straddle Stance position at the feet of Soldier B.
- From the starting position, Soldier A steps over Soldier B, squats, reaching under the armpits and in front of the top of the chest of Soldier B. Soldier A clasps his or her hands together.
- Soldier A stands, leaning or stepping backwards to lift Soldier B backwards until Soldier B's legs are locked straight. Soldier A steps forward to continue to lift Soldier B up onto his or her feet.
- Soldier A separates Soldier B's legs with his or her feet.
- Soldier A lifts one of Soldier B's arms overhead and steps under that arm toward the front of Soldier B and turns to face him or her from the side.
- Soldier A places one leg between and under Soldier B's legs and squats deeply, allowing Soldier B to drape over his or her back.
- Soldier A grasps the back of the far leg of Soldier B and stands up, lifting Soldier B off the ground.
- Soldier A, using the hand of the arm that is between Soldier B's legs, grasps Soldier B's forearm and carries Soldier B at quick time to the 25-meter line.
- After Soldier A places Soldier B's feet back on the ground, the Soldiers switch roles and return to the start.

Figure 6-9. GD3 Soldier Carry

Chapter 7

Running Drills

RUNNING DRILL 1: FOOT STRIKE (RUD1)

7-1.   In running form there are an infinite number of individual differences. The first important difference occurs when the foot strikes the ground. The exercises in Running Drill 1 are one way to improve perception of the way the bodyweight interacts with the ground. Understanding and practicing these drills may help reduce the impact on the Soldier's body and develop running skill.

7-2.   Demonstration videos of Running Drills are located on the Central Army Registry website at https://atiam.train.army.mil/catalog/search?current=true&filetype=mp4&respect_date=5%2F1%2F2020&search_terms=CIMT. (Copy and paste this address after accessing the Central Army Registry website if the demonstrations do not populate.) Additional support for H2F test events and exercises are located on the Army Combat Fitness Test website at https://www.army.mil/acft/.

1. HEEL STRIKE

7-3.   The Heel Strike is the first exercise in Running Drill 1. This exercise increases awareness of the stiffness and locked joints of the leg when the heel strikes the ground first—a rear-foot strike. Figure 7-1 on page 7-2 breaks down the exercise as an individual Soldier conducts it:

- The starting position for the Foot Strike is the Straddle Stance position with hands on hips.
- From the starting position, take an exaggerated step forward with the LEFT leg deliberately landing on the left heel keeping the forefoot off the ground.
- Repeat this exercise 5–10 times.

HEEL STRIKE NOTES

- Take note of the way the heel, ankle, shin, knee, hip, and low back absorb the impact.
- Note how the muscle in the front of the shin keeps the foot off the ground.
- Note how the quadriceps muscle works to lock the knee.
- Note the bend at the hip as the leg reaches out.

Figure 7-1. RUD1.1 Heel Strike

2. HEEL RUN IN PLACE

7-4.   The Heel Run in Place is the second exercise in Running Drill 1. This exercise increases awareness of the braking effect and backwards motion created with a heel strike. Figure 7-2 breaks down the exercise as an individual Soldier conducts it:

- The starting position for the Heel Run in Place is the Straddle Stance position with arms relaxed at the side, knees slightly flexed.
- From the starting position, run in place for 10–15 seconds.
- If conditions permit, repeat without shoes on.

HEEL RUN NOTES

- Note the tendency to move backwards and to lean at the waist to avoid this.
- Note the locked position of the knees.
- Note the impact on the heel, shin, and tension in the low back.
- Note the difference with and without shoes.

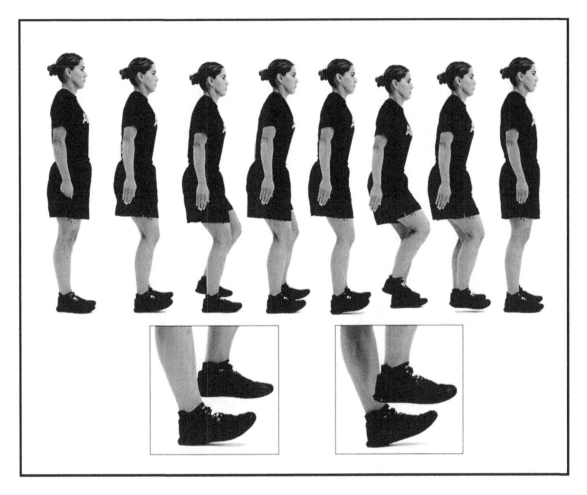

Figure 7-2. RUD1.2 Heel Run in Place

3. 8-COUNT FOOT STRIKE

7-5. The 8-Count Foot Strike increases awareness of ground contact on the whole foot, including the ball of the foot. Figure 7-3 on page 7-4 breaks down the exercise as Soldiers conduct it in formation at slow cadence:

- The starting position for the 8-Count Foot Strike is the Straddle Stance position with hands on hips.
- On count 1, step forward onto the left heel.
- On count 2, allow the left foot to fall flat on the ground.
- On count 3, raise the left heel from the ground.
- On count 4, return to the starting position.
- On count 5, from the starting position, step forward onto the right heel, keeping the right toes off the ground.
- On count 6, allow the right foot to fall flat on the ground.
- On count 7, raise the right heel from the ground.
- On count 8, return to the starting position.
- Repeat this movement 5–10 times before running a short distance or 3–5 seconds.

Figure 7-3. RUD1.3 8-Count Foot Strike

4. RUN IN PLACE 1

7-6.   Run in Place 1 is designed to increase awareness of weight-bearing through the ball of the foot. Figure 7-4 breaks down the exercise as Soldiers conduct it in a formation:

- The starting position for the Run in Place 1 is the Straddle Stance position with arms relaxed at the side.
- Run in place with a ball-of-foot strike for 30 seconds.
- As skill improves, increases the height of the foot pulled from the ground.

RUN IN PLACE 1 NOTES

- Note how the heel slightly touches the ground and does so in a controlled way.
- This form should feel easy, with little effort.
- Note how the knees are bent and springy and are not locked.
- The calf should act like a spring so that you are bouncing, not pushing off the ground.

Figure 7-4. RUD1.4 Run in Place 1

5. RUN IN PLACE 2

7-7.   Run in Place 2 increases awareness of weight-bearing through the ball of the foot. Figure 7-5 breaks down the exercise as Soldiers conduct it in formation:

- The starting position for the Run in Place 2 is the Straddle Stance position with arms relaxed at the side.
- From the starting position, run in place.
- Run in place with a ball-of-foot strike for 30 seconds with and without shoes.
- As skill improves, increases the height of the foot pulled from the ground.

Figure 7-5. RUD1.5 Run in Place 2

RUN IN PLACE 2 NOTES

- Note how the heel slightly touches the ground and does so in a controlled way.
- This form should feel easy, with little effort.
- Note how the knees are bent and springy and are not locked.
- The calf should act like a spring so that you are bouncing, not pushing off the ground.

RUNNING DRILL 2: STRENGTH (RUD2)

7-8.   Running Drill 2 is one way to improve the strength of the muscles needed to prepare the body properly to run.

1. DOUBLE-LEG HOP

7-9.   The Double-Leg Hop is the first exercise in Running Drill 2. This exercise increases the strength of the leg muscles and tendons involved in pulling the feet from the ground. Figure 7-6 breaks down the exercise as an individual Soldier conducts it:

- The starting position is the Straddle Stance position with arms relaxed at the side.
- From the starting position, slightly bend the knees and jump in place. Start with small quick jumps gradually increasing the height and speed as strength improves.
- Repeat this exercise 2–3 times before running a short distance or for 3–5 seconds.

Figure 7-6. RUD2.1 Double-Leg Hop

DOUBLE-LEG HOP NOTES
- When landing, do not allow the knees to come together.
- Keep the knees slightly bent throughout the movement—at take-off and landing.
- Focus on keeping the trunk upright to avoid bending at the waist.

---

2. SINGLE-LEG HOP

7-10.   The Single-Leg Hop is the second exercise in Running Drill 2. This exercise increases the challenge to the muscles and tendons in each leg that assist with pulling. Figure 7-7 breaks down the exercise as an individual Soldier conducts it:

- The starting position is the Straddle Stance position with the right leg pulled up beneath the right hip—the Runner's position.
- From the starting position, hop on the left leg 10 times before pausing to switch legs to repeat the exercise on the left leg.
- Repeat this exercise 2–3 times before running a short distance or for 3–5 seconds.
- Progress to higher pulls as skill improves.

Figure 7-7. RUD2.2 Single-Leg Hop

3. SKIP IN PLACE

7-11. The Skip in Place is the third exercise in Running Drill 2. This exercise increases coordination and the ability to move quickly from support on one foot to another. Figure 7-8 breaks down the exercise as an individual Soldier conducts it:

- The starting position is the Straddle Stance position with arms relaxed at the side.
- From the starting position, skip in place for 3–5 seconds.
- Pause in the starting position before repeating this exercise 2–3 times before running a short distance or for 3–5 seconds.
- Progress to higher skips as skill improves.

Figure 7-8. RUD2.3 Skip in Place

4. TOES IN AND OUT

7-12. The Toes In and Out is the fourth exercise in Running Drill 2. This exercise increases mobility, coordination, and strength in the muscles of the hips and legs. Figure 7-9 breaks down the exercise an individual Soldier conducts it:

- The starting position is the Straddle Stance position.
- From the starting position, jump and land with the feet turned out. Heels should not touch.
- After landing, immediately jump again to land with the feet turned in. Toes should not touch.
- Pause in the starting position before repeating this exercise 2–3 times before running a short distance or for 3–5 seconds.
- Progress to faster cadence and greater rotation of the feet as skill improves.

Figure 7-9. RUD2.4 Toes In and Out

5. CRISS CROSS

7-13. The Criss Cross is the fifth exercise in Running Drill 2. This exercise increases mobility, coordination, and strength in the muscles of the hips and legs in multiple planes of movement. Figure 7-10 breaks down the exercise as an individual Soldier conducts it:

- The starting position is the Straddle Stance position.
- From the starting position, jump while crossing the left foot over the right to land with the feet crossed. Land on the balls of the feet, progressing to the heels.
- Immediately jump again to cross the right foot in front of the left before landing.
- Repeat 5–10 times before pausing in the starting position. Run a short distance or for 3–5 seconds.
- Progress to faster step cadence as skill improves.

Figure 7-10. RUD2.5 Criss Cross

6. PENDULUM

7-14. The Pendulum is the sixth exercise in Running Drill 2. This exercise strengthens muscles of the hips and legs and multi-planar balance and coordination. Figure 7-11 breaks down the exercise as an individual Soldier conducts it:

- The starting position is the Straddle Stance position with arms relaxed at the side.
- From the starting position, swing the left leg out to the side while balancing on the right leg. Keep the left leg straight.
- Bring the left leg back to the starting position before swinging the right leg out to the side.
- Repeat this motion 10 times before pausing in the starting position. Run a short distance or for 3–5 seconds.
- Modify the switch between legs by performing a quick, low hop on the support leg as the swing legs moves back toward the starting position.

Figure 7-11. RUD2.6 Pendulum

7. ALTERNATE TWIST JUMP

7-15. The Alternate Twist Jump is the seventh exercise in Running Drill 2. This exercise strengthens muscles of the hips and legs and multi-planar balance and coordination. Figure 7-12 on page 7-10 breaks down the exercise as an individual Soldier conducts it:

- The starting position is the Straddle Stance position with arms relaxed at the side.
- From the starting position, jump and twist the hips and legs to the left, landing in a staggered stance with the left foot forward.
- Pause before jumping and twisting back to the right to return to the starting position.
- From the starting position, jump and twist the hips and legs to the right, landing in a staggered stance with the right foot forward.
- Pause before jumping and twisting again to the left to return to the starting position.

- Keep the shoulders and head facing forward throughout the movement.
- Progress to completing 5–10 repetitions before running a short distance or for 3–5 seconds.

Figure 7-12. RUD2.7 Alternate Twist Jump

8. HIP RAISE PUSH-UP

7-16. The Hip Raise Push-Up is the eighth exercise in Running Drill 2. This exercise increasingly targets the hip flexor muscles, fatiguing them before short runs so that the pull depends more on hamstring activity. Additionally, this exercise helps increase the perception of falling forward as a single unit, preventing bending at the waist. Figure 7-13 breaks down the exercise as an individual Soldier conducts it:

- The starting position is the Front Leaning Rest position.
- From the starting position, with elbows remaining fully extended, lower the hips toward the ground before quickly moving them back up and into the same flex position used in the Recovery Drill exercise, the Extend and Flex.
- From the flex position, lower the hips toward the ground before quickly moving them back up to the flex position.
- Repeat 10 times before moving into the starting position. Move to the Straddle Stance position before running a short distance or 3–5 seconds.

Figure 7-13. RUD2.8 Hip Raise Push-Up

9. SINGLE-LEG HIP RAISE PUSH-UP

7-17. The Single-Leg Hip Raise Push-Up is the ninth exercise in Running Drill 2. This exercise targets the hip flexor muscles, fatiguing them before short runs so that the pull depends more on hamstring muscle activity. Figure 7-14 breaks down the exercise as an individual Soldier conducts it:

- The starting position is the Front Leaning Rest position with the left foot 8–12 inches off the ground.
- From the starting position, with elbows remaining fully extended and left foot off the ground, lower the hips toward the ground before quickly moving them back up and into the flex position.
- Switch support to the left foot, lifting the right foot 8–12 inches from the ground.
- From the flex position, lower the hips toward the ground before quickly moving them back up to the flex position.
- Continue switching support 5–10 times before moving into the starting position.
- Move to the Straddle Stance position before running a short distance or 3–5 seconds.

Figure 7-14. RUD2.9 Single-Leg Hip Raise Push-Up

10. SINGLE-LEG OUT HIP RAISE PUSH-UP

7-18. The Single-Leg Out Hip Raise Push-Up is the tenth exercise in Running Drill 2. This exercise is an advanced challenge for the hip flexor and extensor muscles. Figure 7-15 on page 7-12 breaks down the exercise as an individual Soldier conducts it:

- The starting position is the Front Leaning Rest position with the left foot 8–12 inches off the ground and held out to the side, or abducted.
- From the starting position, with elbows remaining fully extended, lower the hips toward the ground before quickly moving them back up and into the flex position.
- Switch support to the left foot, abducting and lifting the right foot 8–12 inches from the ground.

- From the flex position, lower the hips toward the ground before quickly moving them back up to the flex position.
- The elevated foot remains off the ground throughout the exercise.
- Continue switching support 5–10 times before moving into the starting position. Move to the Straddle Stance position before running a short distance or 3–5 seconds.

Figure 7-15. RUD2.10 Single-Leg Out Hip Raise Push-Up

RUNNING DRILL 3: RUNNER'S POSITION (RUD3)

7-19. Running Drill 3 is one method to improve the Soldier's ability to move quickly into the Straddle Stance position with the right leg pulled up beneath the right hip—the Runner's position or Pose position. Every runner on every stride goes through this position before he or she takes the next step. The Runner's position precedes the transition to a fall that is necessary to initiate forward motion. Getting into the Runner's position quickly is therefore a key to improved running performance.

1. POSE WEIGHT SHIFT

7-20. Pose Weight Shift is the first exercise in Running Drill 3. This exercise increases perception of the movement to the base of support on the ball of the foot. Figure 7-16 breaks down the exercise as an individual Soldier conducts it:

- The starting position is the Straddle Stance position with arms relaxed at the side.
- From the starting position, pull the right foot from the ground toward the right hip to move into the Runner's position.
- While staying balanced, shift weight backwards and forwards on the left foot while keeping the left heel on the ground.
- The goal of the movement is to remain in Runner's position as far over the front of the foot as possible.
- If you lose balance, move back into the starting position and resume.
- After 2–3 repetitions of 10–15 seconds, switch support to the right foot and repeat.

Figure 7-16. RUD3.1 Pose Weight Shift

2. POSE PULL

7-21. Pose Pull is the second exercise in Running Drill 3. This exercise improves the vertical pull of the foot from the ground, putting the runner back into the Runner's position as quickly as possible. Figure 7-17 on page 7-14 breaks down the exercise as an individual Soldier conducts it:

- The starting position is the Straddle Stance position with arms relaxed at the side.
- From the starting position, pull the left foot from the ground to move into the Runner's position.
- Hold the Runner's position until weight is on the front of the right foot before lowering the left foot back to the ground.
- Repeat this controlled movement 5–10 times before switching to the right side.

Figure 7-17. RUD3.2 Pose Pull

3. ALTERNATE POSE PULL

7-22. The Alternate Pose Pull is the third exercise in Running Drill 3. This is an advanced exercise to improve the speed of the pull into the Runner's position. Figure 7-18 breaks down the exercise as an individual Soldier conducts it:

- The starting position is the Runner's position with support on the left foot.
- From the starting position, pull the left foot from the ground to move into the Runner's position on the right foot.
- Use the support leg as guidance for vertical movement of the foot, not to extend ahead or behind the center of mass, or support.
- As skill improves, increase cadence and reduce the height of the trunk and head movement.
- The goal of the movement is to hold the Runner's position until after the support foot has been pulled from the ground.
- Repeat this movement up to 10 times.

Figure 7-18. RUD3.3 Alternate Pose Pull

RUNNING DRILL 4: FALL (RUD4)

7-23. Falling drills promote the notion that running is not the result of muscular activity; running is the result of gravity accelerating the runner forward. No strength is required to fall. These drills are designed to build confidence that Soldiers must fall freely to initiate movement. As a runner falls, gravity accelerates the runner forward from the Runner's position. This drill enhances the feeling of acceleration to improve running skill.

1. TIMBER FALL

7-24. The Timber Fall is the first exercise in Running Drill 4. This exercise improves perception of how little effort is required to move forward. Figure 7-19 on page 7-16 shows the exercise as an individual Soldier conducts it:

- The starting position for the Timber Fall is the Straddle Stance position with arms relaxed at the side, knees slightly flexed.
- From the starting position, shift weight to the balls of the feet. Avoid bending at the waist and initiate a fall. Prevent falling to the ground by taking a short step forward with the left foot. Return to the start position.
- Repeat this movement 5–10 times onto each foot before running a short distance or 3–5 seconds.

Figure 7-19. RUD4.1 Timber Fall

2. TIMBER FALL IN POSE

7-25. Timber Fall in Pose is the second exercise in Running Drill 4. This exercise progresses the Soldier's perception of how to move forward from the dominant running position. Figure 7-20 breaks down the exercise as an individual Soldier conducts it:

- The starting position for the Timber Fall in Pose is the Straddle Stance position with arms relaxed at the side, knees slightly flexed.
- From the starting position, pull the left foot from the ground directly under the hip. While maintaining this running pose, shift body weight to the ball of the foot and initiate a fall. Prevent falling to the ground by placing the left foot on the ground. Return to the starting position.
- Repeat this movement 5–10 times onto each foot before running a short distance or 3–5 seconds.

Figure 7-20. RUD4.2 Timber Fall in Pose

3. WALL FALL

7-26. The Wall Fall is the third exercise in Running Drill 4. This exercise promotes the tendency to resist falling. Figure 7-21 breaks down the exercise as an individual Soldier conducts it:

- The starting position for the Wall Fall is the Straddle Stance position with hands ahead of the body and two feet from the wall.
- From the starting position, fall into the wall while maintaining the same body position throughout the fall. Use the hands and arms to stop the fall. Do not bend at the waist. Keep the heels on the ground and keep the knees slightly flexed. Return to the starting position.
- Repeat this movement 5–10 times before running a short distance or 3–5 seconds.

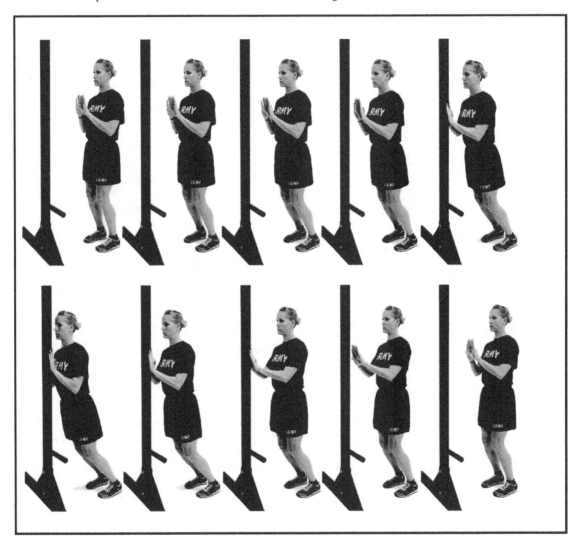

Figure 7-21. RUD4.3 Wall Fall

4. WALL FALL IN POSE

7-27. The Wall Fall in Pose is the fourth exercise in Running Drill 4. This exercise promotes the tendency to resist falling from the Runner's position. Figure 7-22 breaks down the exercise as an individual Soldier conducts it:

- The starting position for the Wall Fall is the Straddle Stance position with hands ahead of the body and two feet from the wall.
- From the starting position, pull the left foot from the ground directly under the hip into the Runner's position. While maintaining this position, shift body weight to the ball of the foot and initiate a fall. Use the hands and arms to stop the fall. Return to the starting position.
- Repeat this movement 5–10 times onto each foot before running a short distance or 3–5 seconds.

Figure 7-22. RUD4.4 Wall Fall in Pose

5. STRETCH CORD FALL

7-28. The Stretch Cord Fall is the fifth exercise in Running Drill 4. By providing extra support at the hips, this exercise promotes the ability to fall without bending at the waist. If the runner is unable to fall, or has a fear of falling, he or she will bend at the waist to keep the center of mass over the base of support. Figure 7-23 breaks down the exercise as an individual Soldier conducts it:

- The starting position for the Stretch Cord Fall is the Straddle Stance position with arms relaxed at the sides, reflective belt or elastic band around the front of the runner's hips. The partner stands behind the runner pulling tension on the belt or tubing.
- From the starting position, the runner slowly falls forward maintaining body position while the partner provides support to prevent the runner from falling down. Return to the starting position.
- Repeat this movement 5–10 times before running a short distance or 3–5 seconds.

Figure 7-23. RUD4.5 Stretch Cord Fall

6. PARTNER ASSISTED FALL

7-29. The Partner Assisted Fall is the sixth exercise in Running Drill 4. This exercise improves the ability to fall without bending at the waist by providing extra support at the shoulders. Figure 7-24 breaks down the exercise as an individual Soldier conducts it:

- The starting position for the Partner Assisted Fall for the runner is the Straddle Stance position with arms relaxed at the sides. The partner places both hands on the runner's shoulders ready to provide support.
- From the starting position, the runner pulls the left foot from the ground directly under the hip into the Runner's position.
- While maintaining this pose, shift body weight to the ball of the foot and initiate a fall. The partner holds the runner during the fall.
- Repeat this movement 5–10 times until releasing the runner to run a short distance or 3–5 seconds.

Figure 7-24. RUD4.6 Partner Assisted Fall

7. KNEELING TIMBER FALL

7-30. The Kneeling Timber Fall is the seventh exercise in Running Drill 4. This exercise increases hamstring strength and the awareness of trunk stability during the fall. Figure 7-25 breaks down the exercise as an individual Soldier conducts it:

- The starting position for the runner in the Kneeling Timber Fall is the kneeling position with hands held in front, ready to absorb impact with the ground. The partner squats behind the runner and holds down the runner's heels or lower legs. The runner's knees will be on a cushioned surface.
- From the starting position, the runner falls to the ground while maintaining the same body position and avoiding bending at the waist.
- The runner catches himself or herself before hitting the ground. The partner holds the runner during the fall.
- Repeat this movement up to 5 times and then run a short distance or 3–5 seconds.

Figure 7-25. RUD4.7 Kneeling Timber Fall

8. SPRINT START

7-31. The Sprint Start is the final exercise in Running Drill 4. This exercise promotes the feeling of an extreme fall angle, and the difference between falling and pushing from the ground in order to run. Figure 7-26 breaks down the exercise as an individual Soldier conducts it:

- The starting position for the Sprint Start is the Front Leaning Rest with the left leg under the chest and the right knee under the hip.
- From the starting position, place as much body weight on your hands as possible.
- First, pull both hands from the ground to initiate a fall.
- Immediately move the right leg under the body to regain the base of support.
- Move rapidly into the upright running position.
- Repeat this movement up to 5 times before running a short distance or 3–5 seconds.

SPRINT START NOTES

- Note how hard it is to lift the hands first—there is a fear of falling.
- Note how fast you move without needing to push with the legs.
- Note how the right foot quickly and automatically pulls up and regains support.

Figure 7-26. RUD4.8 Sprint Start

RUNNING DRILL 5: PULL (RUD5)

7-32. Running Drill 5 improves the Soldier's ability to increase running efficiency. Pulling drills reduce impact force as the foot is quickly pulled from the ground and back into the Runner's position.

1. WALK PROGRESSION

7-33. The Walk Progression is the first exercise in Running Drill 5. This exercise improves awareness of how speed increases when the foot spends less time on the ground. It also illustrates the fact that "striding out" is not a technique to increase speed or efficiency. Figure 7-27 breaks down the exercise as an individual Soldier conducts it:

- The starting position is the Straddle Stance position with arms relaxed at the side.
- From the starting position, the Soldier walks quickly forward using long strides and heel striking, increasing speed until he or she can no longer walk, but wants to start running.
- Repeat this exercise 2–3 times over a short distance or 3–5 seconds.

WALK PROGRESSION NOTES
- Note how the walking strides become shorter as the speed increases.
- Note how longer strides require more time on support—more ground contact.
- Note the switch heel to forefoot support as speed increases.

Figure 7-27. RUD5.1 Walk Progression

2. PONY

7-34. The Pony is the second exercise in Running Drill 5. This exercise improves the awareness of the location of support and reduces the length of time on support. Figure 7-28 breaks down the exercise as an individual Soldier conducts it:

- The starting position is the Straddle Stance position with arms relaxed at the side.
- From the starting position, raise up onto the ball of the left foot.
- Switch back and forth between left and right feet increasing the cadence to a minimum of 180 steps per minute.
- Repeat this exercise 2–3 times before running a short distance.

PONY NOTES

- Note how much easier it is to perform as the foot pulls off the ground at a higher rate.
- Note how the whole body unweights as speed and skill improves.

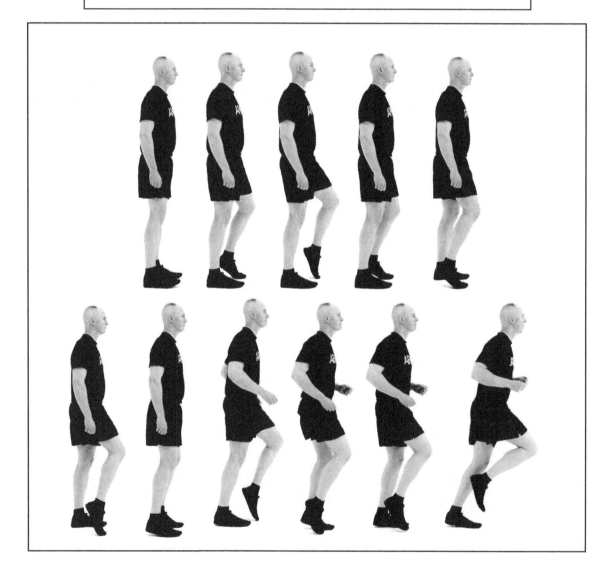

Figure 7-28. RUD5.2 Pony

3. PULL BACK

7-35. The Pull Back is the third exercise in Running Drill 5. This exercise improves the perception of the pull and of keeping the pulled limb relaxed. Figure 7-29 breaks down the exercise as an individual Soldier conducts it:

- The starting position is the Straddle Stance position with staggered legs and arms relaxed at the side. Body weight is equally distributed between the feet.
- From the starting position, the Soldier pulls the left foot off the ground. This is a quick, forceful motion.
- The body stays in place exerting only a pulling effort without a push as the foot leaves the ground.
- Repeat this exercise 5–10 times on each leg before running a short distance.

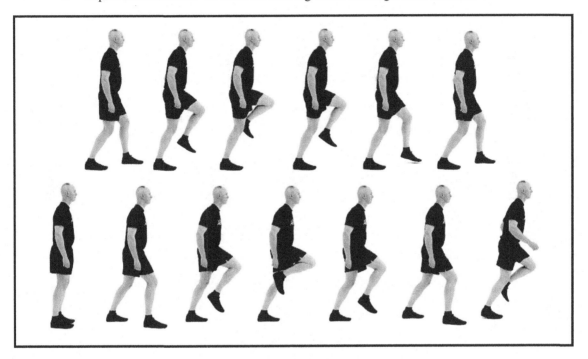

Figure 7-29. RUD5.3 Pull Back

4. ELEVATED PULL BACK

7-36. The Elevated Pull Back is the fourth exercise in Running Drill 5. This exercise improves the perception of the pull and of keeping the pulled limb relaxed. Figure 7-30 breaks down the exercise as an individual Soldier conducts it:

- The starting position is the Straddle Stance position with staggered legs, arms relaxed at the side, and the right foot resting on a step stool. Most of the body weight is on the left foot.
- From the starting position, the Soldier pulls the left foot off the ground. This is a quick, forceful motion. The right foot rests on the step stool.
- The body stays in place when there only pulling effort without a push as the foot leaves the ground.
- Repeat this exercise 5–10 times on each leg before running a short distance.

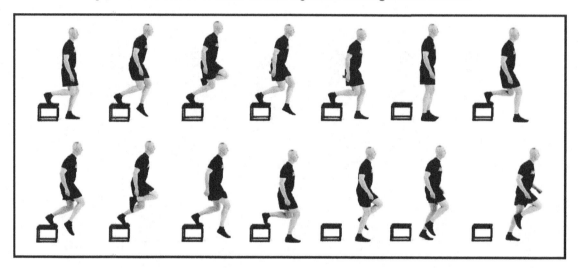

Figure 7-30. RUD5.4 Elevated Pull Back

5. KICK START

7-37. The Kick Start is the fifth exercise in Running Drill 5. This exercise improves the accuracy of the pull and facilitates hamstring activity prior to running. Figure 7-31 breaks down the exercise as an individual Soldier conducts it with a partner to assist:

- The starting position for the runner is the Straddle Stance position with arms relaxed at the side. The partner (or coach) stands with hands on the runner's shoulders and the left foot resting against the runner's left heel.
- From the starting position, the runner pulls the left foot straight up under the hip. The partner provides gentle resistance against the movement.
- Repeat the movement 5–10 times on each leg before running a short distance.

Figure 7-31. RUD5.5 Kick Start

RUNNING DRILL 6: COMBINATIONS (RUD6)

7-38. Running Drill 6 challenges the runner's ability to combine lessons of the previous running drills into a smooth, sustained run.

1. CHANGE OF SUPPORT

7-39. The Change of Support is the first exercise in Running Drill 6. This exercise increases the perception of falling from the Runner's position. Figure 7-34 shows the exercise as an individual Soldier conducts it:

- The starting position for the Change of Support is the Runner's position with hands in the ready position against the wall. The left leg is the support leg.
- From the starting position, with hands on the wall, pull the support leg from the ground.
- Focus on pulling the support leg prior to lowering the right leg.
- Repeat this exercise up to 5 times on both sides before running a short distance or 3–5 seconds.

Figure 7-34. RUD6.1 Change of Support

2. HOP IN PLACE

7-40. The Hop in Place is the second exercise in Running Drill 6. This exercise increases the speed of the pull and improves the ability to remain in the Runner's position throughout the fall. Figure 7-35 breaks down the exercise as an individual Soldier conducts it:

- The starting position for the Hop in Place is the Runner's position. The left leg is the support leg.
- From the starting position, pull the support leg from the ground. To avoid pushing, concentrate on keeping the head and upper body in same place.
- Repeat 5–10 times on both legs before running a short distance or 3–5 seconds.

Figure 7-35. RUD6.2 Hop in Place

3. HOP FORWARD

7-41. The Hop Forward is the third exercise in Running Drill 6. This exercise prevents bending at the waist. Figure 7-36 breaks down the exercise as an individual Soldier conducts it:

- The starting position for the Hop Forward is the Runner's position.
- From the starting position, hop from one foot to the other in place before progressing forward by hopping for a short distance or 3–5 seconds.
- After completing the drill, run a short distance or for 3–5 seconds.

Figure 7-36. RUD6.3 Hop Forward

4. RUN IN POSE

7-42. The Run in Pose is the fourth exercise in Running Drill 6. This exercise increases the ability to run more efficiently. Figure 7-37 breaks down the exercise as an individual Soldier conducts it:

- The starting position for the Run in Pose is the Runner's position.
- From the starting position, run in place at 3 steps per second—180 steps per minute.
- Fall forward to initiate the run and run at moderate speed for a short distance or 3–5 seconds.

Figure 7-37. RUD6.4 Run in Pose

5. BACKWARDS RUN

7-43. The Backwards Run is the final exercise in Running Drill 6. This exercise increases the perception of gravity during the fall—Soldiers will feel how easy it is to let gravity do the work of moving them when they run backwards. Figure 7-38 on page 7-30 breaks down the exercise as an individual Soldier conducts it:

- The starting position is the Straddle Stance position. The runner runs in place at 180 steps per minute.
- After a few seconds, initiate a backwards fall and run backwards for a short distance. At that point and without stopping, turn around and run forward for 3–5 seconds.
- Repeat this exercise up to 5 times.

Figure 7-38. RUD6.5 Backwards Run

RUNNING DRILL 7: CORRECTIONS (RUD7)

7-44. In the training of every Soldier, nothing equals the importance of proper skill. Correction exercises are used to improve running skill by correcting improper form.

1. HANDS IN FRONT

7-45. Hands in Front is the first exercise in Running Drill 7 (see figure 7-39). This exercise brings the trunk into a more upright position. It improves the perception of trunk position and increases awareness of the tendency to lean from the waist as an individual Soldier makes the following moves:

- The starting position for the Hands in Front is the Runner's position with arms straight out in front of the body from the shoulder, hands clasped together.
- From the starting position, run a short distance or 3–5 seconds.
- Repeat this exercise up to 5 times before running a short distance without Hands in Front.

Figure 7-39. RUD7.1 Hands in Front

2. HANDS BEHIND

7-46. The Hands Behind is the second exercise in Running Drill 7. This exercise brings the trunk into a more upright position, improves the perception of trunk position, and increases awareness of the tendency to lean from the waist. In this drill, the Soldier will feel pushed into leaning and will have to resist. Figure 7-40 breaks down the exercise as an individual Soldier conducts it:

- The starting position for the Hands Behind is the Runner's position with arms behind the back hands clasped together.
- From the starting position, run a short distance or 3–5 seconds.
- Repeat this exercise up to 5 times before running a short distance without Hands Behind.

Figure 7-40. RUD7.2 Hands Behind

3. HANDS ON BACK

7-47. The Hands on Back is the third exercise in Running Drill 7. This exercise prevents bending at the waist. Figure 7-41 breaks down the exercise as an individual Soldier conducts it:

- The starting position for the Hands on Back is the Runner's position with the hands placed on the small of the back.
- From the starting position, run a short distance or 3–5 seconds.
- Repeat this movement up to 5 times before running a short distance or 3–5 seconds without the hands on the back.

Figure 7-41. RUD7.3 Hands on Back

4. HANDS ON BELLY

7-48. The Hands on Belly is the fourth exercise in Running Drill 7. This exercise increases the awareness of falling and not bending at the waist. Figure 7-42 breaks down the exercise as an individual Soldier conducts it:

- The starting position for the Hands on Belly is the Runner's position with the hands on the belly.
- From the starting position, run a short distance or 3–5 seconds.
- Repeat this movement up to 5 times before running a short distance or 3–5 seconds without the hands on the belly.

Figure 7-42. RUD7.4 Hands on Belly

5. SHIN BURN

7-49. The Shin Burn is the fifth exercise in Running Drill 7. This exercise reduces the tendency to heel strike by fatiguing the muscle that supports the heel strike. Figure 7-43 breaks down the exercise as an individual Soldier conducts it with a coach or partner to assist:

- The starting position for the runner is the Straddle Stance position with staggered legs and arms relaxed at the side. The partner kneels to the front left side of the runner, with one hand on the top of the runner's left foot and the other hand on the back of the runner's left knee to prevent knee extension.
- From the starting position, the runner raises the left foot while the partner holds the foot down.
- Repeat this movement up to 5 times on each foot before running a short distance or 3–5 seconds.

Figure 7-43. RUD7.5 Shin Burn

6. INFANTRY RUN

7-50. The Infantry Run is the sixth exercise in Running Drill 7. This exercise applies skills learned in the previous Running Drills with assistance of feedback from a partner. It is best conducted around the physical training track in intervals such as the 30:60s or 60:120s. Figure 7-44 breaks down the exercise as an individual Soldier conducts it:

- The starting position for the runner is the Runner's position. For the partner, the starting position is standing behind the runner also in the Runner's position with hands on the runner's shoulders.
- From the starting position, both Soldiers run in place at the same cadence—3 steps per second—until the lead runner initiates a run.
- Repeat around a physical training track at speed that allow both Soldiers to stay in step.

Figure 7-44. RUD7.6 Infantry Run

7. BATTLE BUDDY

7-51. The Battle Buddy is the seventh exercise in Running Drill 7. This exercise applies skills learned in the previous Running Drills with assistance of feedback from a partner. It is best conducted around the physical training track in intervals such as the 30:60s or 60:120s. Figure 7-45 breaks down the exercise as an individual Soldier conducts it:

- The starting position for the runner is the Runner's position. For the partner, the starting position is standing shoulder to shoulder next to the runner also in the Runner's position.
- From the starting position, begin running in place at the same cadence of 3 steps per second until the lead runner initiates a run. Run elbow to elbow for a short distance or 3–5 seconds.
- Repeat this movement up to 5 times before running around a physical training track for intervals and speeds that allow both Soldiers to stay in step.

Figure 7-45. RUD7.7 Battle Buddy

Chapter 8

Military Movement Drills

MILITARY MOVEMENT DRILL 1 (MMD1)

8-1.   Military Movement Drill 1 is a dynamic preparation activity for the more vigorous endurance and mobility activities in physical training. It develops motor coordination in multiple planes for foot movement at varying speeds over the ground.

8-2.   Videos of Military Movement Drills located on the Central Army Registry website at https://atiam.train.army.mil/catalog/search?current=true&filetype=mp4&respect_date=5%2F1%2F2020&search_terms=CIMT demonstrate movements. (Copy and paste this address after accessing the Central Army Registry website if the demonstrations do not populate.) Additional support for H2F test events and exercises are located on the Army Combat Fitness Test website at https://www.army.mil/acft/.

1. VERTICAL

8-3.   The Vertical is the first exercise in Military Movement Drill 1. This exercise improves single leg jumping and landing skill in preparation for more vigorous training, testing, and combat activities. Figure 8-1 breaks down the exercise as an individual Soldier conducts it:

- The starting position is the Straddle Stance position with staggered legs with the right foot forward. The right heel is even with the toes of the left foot. The head is up looking straight ahead and the knees are slightly bent. The left arm is forward.
- From the starting position, swing the left thigh up to 90 degrees and the right arm forward before stepping forward with the left foot.
- As the left foot comes to the ground, raise the right thigh to 90 degrees and the left arm forward before stepping forward with the right foot.
- Repeat this motion down a 25-meter course before stopping. Repeat once to return to the start line.

Figure 8-1. MMD1.1 Vertical

2. LATERAL

8-4.   The Lateral is the second exercise in Military Movement Drill 1. It is the third leg of the Sprint-Drag-Carry event in the ACFT. This exercise develops the ability to move laterally in preparation for more vigorous training, testing, and combat activities. Figure 8-2 shows the exercise as an individual Soldier conducts it:

- The starting position is the Straddle Stance, with left side facing the direction of movement. Crouch slightly with elbows bent to 90 degrees and palms facing forward.
- From the starting position, step out with the lead leg and then bring the trail leg up and toward the lead leg.
- The Soldier always faces the same direction so that the for the first 25 meters he or she is moving to the left and for the second 25 meters is moving to the right.
- As skill improves, the Soldier may increase speed.

Figure 8-2. MMD1.2 Lateral

3. SHUTTLE SPRINT

8-5.   The Shuttle Sprint is the third exercise in Military Movement Drill 1. This exercise prepares the Soldier for more vigorous endurance and agility activities. Figure 8-3 breaks down the exercise as an individual Soldier conducts it:

- The starting position is the Straddle Stance position with staggered legs, with the right foot forward. The right heel is even with the toes of the left foot. The head is up looking straight ahead and the knees are slightly bent. The left arm is forward.
- From the starting position, run quickly to the 25-meter turn-around point.
- Turn clockwise while planting the left foot and bending and squatting to touch the ground with the left hand.
- Run quickly back to the starting line and plant the right foot, then turn counter-clockwise and touch the ground with the right hand.
- Run back to the 25-meter turn-around accelerating to maximum speed through the finish.

Figure 8-3. MMD1.3 Shuttle Sprint

MILITARY MOVEMENT DRILL 2 (MMD2)

8-6. Military Movement Drill 2 is a dynamic preparation drill for the plyometric movements required in Conditioning Drill 3, obstacle course negotiation, Terrain Runs, and other multi-planar movements encountered in combat tasks.

1. POWER SKIP

8-7. The Power Skip is the first exercise in Military Movement Drill 2. This exercise develops powerful single-leg vertical jumping and landing skill in preparation for more vigorous testing and combat activities. Figure 8-4 on page 8-4 breaks down the exercise as Soldiers conduct it in a formation:

- The starting position is the Straddle Stance position with staggered legs with the right foot forward. The right heel is even with the toes of the left foot. The head is up looking straight ahead and the knees are slightly bent. The left arm is forward.
- From the starting position, step with the left foot then skip powerfully up from the ground with the right leg.
- As the right leg moves up, the left arm swings powerfully forward and up. The right arm counter-moves to the rear.
- After landing on the left leg, immediately repeat the skip movement, leading with the left leg.
- When the left leg is forward, the right arm drives up and forward to unweight the body as it leaves the ground.
- Repeat this motion down a 25-meter course before stopping. Repeat once to return to the start line.
- As skill improves, the Soldier may increase height of the skip.

Figure 8-4. MMD2.1 Power Skip

2. CROSSOVER

8-8.   The Crossover is the second exercise in Military Movement Drill 2. This exercise develops leg coordination and trains Soldiers to move laterally. Figure 8-5 breaks down the exercise as Soldiers conduct it in formation:

- The starting position is the Straddle Stance, slightly crouched with the back straight, arms at the side with elbows bent at 90 degrees. Palms face forward. The body is turned so that the left side faces the 25-meter course.
- From the starting position, cross the trail leg in front of the lead leg to complete the first lateral step.
- On the second lateral step, cross the trail leg behind the lead leg to uncross the legs.
- On the third step, cross the trail leg behind the lead leg.
- On the fourth step cross the trail leg in front of the lead leg to uncross the legs.
- This four-step pattern repeats down the 25-meter course.
- Pick the feet up, moving from the ball of the foot, and increasing lateral speed as skill improves.
- Maintain a crouch throughout the movement and keep the back straight and trunk perpendicular to the direction of movement.
- Repeat once back down the 25-meter course to return to the start line.

Figure 8-5. MMD2.2 Crossover

3. CROUCH RUN

8-9.   The Crouch Run is the third exercise in Military Movement Drill 2. This exercise develops the ability to run quickly in a crouched position. Figure 8-6 on page 8-6 breaks down the exercise as Soldiers conduct it in formation:

- The starting position is the starting position for the Mountain Climber exercise (see paragraph 5-5).
- From the starting position, complete one 4-count repetition of the Mountain Climber before running forward in a crouched position down the 25-meter course.
- The arms move minimally, as though carrying a weapon.
- At the end of the 25-meter course, turn clockwise while planting the left foot, bending and squatting to touch the ground with the left hand.
- Crouch run quickly back to the start line.
- At the start of the 25-meter course, turn counter-clockwise planting the right foot, bending and squatting to touch the ground with the right hand.
- Maintain a crouch throughout the turn before accelerating to an upright run at maximal speed though the end of the 25-meter course.
- Repeat once to return to the start of the 25-meter course.

Figure 8-6. MMD2.3 Crouch Run

Chapter 9

Medicine Ball Drills

MEDICINE BALL DRILL 1 (MB1)

9-1. Medicine Ball Drill 1 (known as MB1) is a dynamic preparation drill consisting of five exercises conducted in multiple planes. A medicine ball of appropriate size and weight for the session provides light resistance. Medicine Ball Drill 1 prepares the body for advanced conditioning and strengthening drills as well as more vigorous physical test events and combat tasks.

9-2. Demonstration videos of Medicine Ball Drills are located on the Central Army Registry website at https://atiam.train.army.mil/catalog/search?current=true&filetype=mp4&respect_date=5%2F1%2F2020&s earch_terms=CIMT. (Copy and paste this address after accessing the Central Army Registry website if the demonstrations do not populate.) Additional support for H2F test events and exercises are located on the Army Combat Fitness Test website at https://www.army.mil/acft/.

1. CHEST PASS LATERAL

9-3. The Chest Pass Lateral is the first exercise in Medicine Ball Drill 1. It requires a wall to throw against and a medicine ball of size and weight suitable to meet the physical training session's goal. Figure 9-1 breaks down the exercise as an individual Soldier conducts it using a four-count movement:

- The starting position for the Chest Pass Lateral is the Straddle Stance position with ball held in front of the chest, ready to throw forward.
- The ball is thrown from a distance that allows the ball to rebound into the Soldier's hands.
- On count 1, from the starting position, the Soldier throws the ball at the wall while simultaneously stepping laterally to the left.
- The lateral step happens while the ball is going to and from the wall.
- On count 2, repeat count 1, stepping laterally to the right to return to the starting position.
- On count 3, repeat count 1, once more stepping laterally to the right.
- On count 4, repeat count 1, stepping laterally to the left to return to the starting position.

Figure 9-1. MB1.1 Chest Pass Lateral

2. ALTERNATING SIDE-ARM THROW

9-4.   The Alternating Side-Arm Throw is the second exercise in Medicine Ball Drill 1. It requires a wall to throw against and a medicine ball of size and weight suitable to meet the physical training session's goal. Figure 9-2 breaks down the exercise as an individual Soldier conducts it using a four-count movement:

- The starting position for the Alternating Side-Arm Throw is the Straddle Stance position with feet wider than shoulder width, and the ball held to the right of the waist, ready to throw sideways to the left. The Soldier's left side faces the wall.
- The ball is thrown from a distance that allows the ball to rebound into the Soldier's hands.
- On count 1, from the starting position, throw the ball at the wall from right to the left while simultaneously rotating to face the wall in preparation to catch it.
- On count 2, catch the ball, stepping and rotating the trunk arms and shoulders to the left to absorb the ball's weight.
- On count 3, repeat count 1, this time throwing from left to right.
- On count 4, repeat count 2, stepping and rotating the trunk arms and shoulders to the right to absorb the ball's weight to return to the starting position.

Figure 9-2. MB1.2 Alternating Side-Arm Throw

3. DIAGONAL CHOP

9-5.   The Diagonal Chop is the third exercise in Medicine Ball Drill 1. It requires medicine ball of size and weight suitable to meet the physical training session's goal. Figure 9-3 breaks down the exercise as an individual Soldier conducts it using a four-count movement at a slow cadence:

- The starting position for the Diagonal Chop is the Straddle Stance position with ball held in front of the waist.
- On count 1, from the starting position, move the ball high above the left shoulder.
- On count 2, move the ball down and to the right, simultaneously squatting so that the ball reaches a point to the side of the right knee.
- On count 3, move from the count 2 position to the count 1 position—moving the ball high above the left shoulder.
- On count 4, return to the starting position.
- The second 4-count repetition switches the diagonal pattern to the opposite side.
- On count 1, move the ball high above the right shoulder.
- On count 2, move the ball down to the left knee.
- On count 3, move the ball back to the count 1 position.
- On count 4, return to the starting position.
- The exercise continues this alternating pattern for 5–10 repetitions on each side.

Figure 9-3. MB1.3 Diagonal Chop

4. SLAM

9-6.   The Slam is the fourth exercise in Medicine Ball Drill 1. It requires a medicine ball of size and weight suitable to meet the physical training session's goal. A slam ball is recommended to prevent too much movement of the ball after it hits the ground. Figure 9-4 on page 9-4 breaks down the exercise as an individual Soldier conducts it using a four-count movement:

- The starting position for the Slam is the Straddle Stance position with ball held in front of the waist.
- On count 1, from the starting position, lift the ball up and over the head.
- On count 2, perform a slight squat while forcefully throwing the ball to the ground with both arms just in front of the feet.
- On count 3, squat down to pick the ball up.
- On count 4, return to the starting position.
- Complete this exercise 5–10 times.
- As skill improves, the Soldier may add more power to the movement by jumping during the throw.

Figure 9-4. MB1.4 Slam

5. UNDERHAND WALL THROW

9-7. The Underhand Wall Throw is the fifth exercise in Medicine Ball Drill 1. It requires a wall and a medicine ball of size and weight suitable to meet the physical training session's goal. Figure 9-5 breaks down the exercise as an individual Soldier conducts it using a four-count movement:

- The starting position for the Underhand Wall Throw is the Straddle Stance position with ball held in front of the waist.
- On count 1, from the starting position, squat to lower the ball between the legs and toward the rear. This is the same position used in count 1 of Bend and Reach exercise (see paragraph 3-3).
- On count 2, using an underhand motion, forcefully throw the ball at the wall, aiming for a point on the wall that allows for a rebound and waist-high catch.
- On count 3, continue the catch motion, absorbing the weight of the ball by squatting to lower the ball between the legs.
- On count 4, without pausing the movement of the ball begun in count 3, move quickly through the count 1 squat position to throw the ball again.
- Do not return to the starting position until completion of the final repetition.
- Maintain proper squat posture with the spine straight throughout the exercise.
- Note that the power for the throw derives from the movement of the hips as body weight is shifted over the feet.
- Complete this exercise 5–10 times, returning to the starting position after the final repetition.

Figure 9-5. MB1.5 Underhand Wall Throw

MEDICINE BALL DRILL 2 (MB2)

9-8. Medicine Ball Drill 2 (known as MB2) is an advanced resistance drill consisting of five medicine ball exercises conducted in multiple planes. Heavier medicine balls can be used in Medicine Ball Drill 2 to make it an alternative to Free Weight Assistive exercises. Medicine Ball Drill 2 can also substitute for or supplement advanced conditioning and strengthening drills when free weight equipment is not available or when conditions are not suitable.

1. DIAGONAL CHOP THROW

9-9. The Diagonal Chop Throw is the first exercise in Medicine Ball Drill 2. It requires a medicine ball of size and weight suitable to meet the physical training session's goal. Figure 9-6 on page 9-6 breaks down the exercise as a Soldier conducts it using a four-count movement and a slam ball or wall to reduce the rolling distance:

- The starting position for the Diagonal Chop is the Straddle Stance position with ball held in front of the waist.
- On count 1, from the starting position, move the ball high above the left shoulder.
- On count 2, throw the ball to the ground aiming to the right of the right foot.
- After retrieving the ball, on count 3, repeat count 1, this time moving the ball high above the right shoulder.
- On count 4, repeat count 2, throwing the ball to the left of the left foot.

Figure 9-6. MB2.1 Diagonal Chop Throw

2. KNEELING SIDE-ARM THROW

9-10. The Kneeling Side-Arm Throw is the second exercise in Medicine Ball Drill 2. It requires a wall or partner to throw to and a medicine ball of size and weight suitable to meet the physical training session's goal. Figure 9-7 illustrates the exercise as a Soldier with a partner conducts it:

- The starting position for the Kneeling Side-Arm Throw is the Half-Kneeling position on the left knee. The ball is held at the waist, ready to throw from right to left. The left side of the body faces the partner.
- From the starting position, throw the ball to the partner from right to the left.
- The catching Soldier absorbs the impact by catching it with an exaggerated rotation of the arms, shoulders, and trunk to the right.
- Alternatively, the catch can be made by deliberately resisting trunk rotation, in which case the arms absorb the impact.

Figure 9-7. MB2.2 Kneeling Side-Arm Throw

3. SUMO WALL THROW

9-11. The Sumo Wall Throw is the third exercise in Medicine Ball Drill 2. It requires a wall to throw against and a medicine ball of size and weight suitable to meet the physical training session's goal. Figure 9-8 breaks down the exercise as an individual Soldier using a two-count movement conducts it:

- The starting position for the Sumo Wall Throw is the Straddle Stance position with feet slightly wider than shoulder width apart, ready to perform a Sumo squat. The ball is held in front of the chest, ready to throw forward.
- On count 1, from the starting position, squat deeply, widening foot stance and turning the feet out to perform a deep Sumo squat. Move elbows between the knees with ball held in position in front of the chest.
- On count 2, power up and out of the squat, pushing the ball up overhead to throw it high up on the wall.
- Allow the ball to fall to the ground.
- After retrieving the ball, repeat counts 1 and 2 for 5–10 repetitions.

Figure 9-8. MB2.3 Sumo Wall Throw

4. SIT-UP THROW

9-12. The Sit-Up Throw is the fourth exercise in Medicine Ball Drill 2. It requires a wall or partner to throw to and a medicine ball of size and weight suitable to meet the physical training session's goal. Figure 9-9 breaks down the exercise as a Soldier and a partner conduct it:

- The starting position for the Sit-Up Throw is the Supine position, with feet flat on the ground and knees bent to 90 degrees. Feet are toward the partner. The ball is held on the chest with both hands, ready to throw toward the partner.
- The weight of the ball and the distance from the partner is calibrated so that the Soldiers can catch and throw to each other.
- From the starting position, the Soldier flexes the trunk and hips in a sit-up motion, while simultaneously pushing the ball up and toward the partner.
- The partner catches the ball in both hands, absorbing the impact by bending the elbows and leaning backwards in the trunk to return to the starting position.
- Both Soldiers keep their feet on the ground throughout the exercise.
- When a wall is available, the ball must be thrown with enough force to rebound back to the Soldier.

Figure 9-9. MB2.4 Sit-Up Throw

5. RAINBOW SLAM

9-13. The Rainbow Slam is the fifth exercise in Medicine Ball Drill 2. It requires a medicine ball of size and weight suitable to meet the physical training session's goal. Figure 9-10 breaks down the exercise as an individual Soldier conducts it:

- The starting position for the Rainbow Slam is the Straddle Stance position with the ball held at waist height.
- From the starting position, move the ball up and to the left and then in an arc to the right.
- While turning to the right, begin a forceful throw directing the ball to the ground.
- Retrieve the ball before repeating the exercise in the opposite direction.
- Complete this exercise 5–10 times on each side.
- As skill improves, add more power to the throw by jumping during the throwing motion.

Figure 9-10. MB2.5 Rainbow Slam

This page intentionally left blank.

Chapter 10

Suspension Training Drills

SUSPENSION TRAINING DRILL 1 (ST1)

10-1. Suspension Training Drill 1 (known as ST1) is a series of five exercises using straps suspended from various types of anchor points to train the whole body. Suspension Training Drill 1 exercises, when conducted in the correct order and correct number of repetitions, provide a moderate muscular endurance challenge to supplement other physical training conditioning drills. When used with Suspension Drill 2, Suspension Training Drill 1 exercises prepare the body for more vigorous physical training and test events.

10-2. Videos of Suspension Training Drills located on the Central Army Registry website at https://atiam.train.army.mil/catalog/search?current=true&filetype=mp4&respect_date=5%2F1%2F2020&search_terms=CIMT demonstrate movements. (Copy and paste this address after accessing the Central Army Registry website if the demonstrations do not populate.) Additional support for H2F test events and exercises are located on the Army Combat Fitness Test website at https://www.army.mil/acft/.

1. SUSPENSION PUSH-UP

10-3. The Suspension Push-Up is the first exercise in Suspension Training Drill 1. It challenges shoulder stability by suspending either the feet or the hands above the ground. Figure 10-1 breaks down the exercise as conducted by an individual Soldier with the hands suspended above the ground:

- The starting position for the Suspension Push-Up is the Front Leaning Rest position, with hands in the straps suspended from the ground. Elbows are fully extended and feet are no more than shoulder width apart on the ground.
- The Soldier may adjust the straps that incline the Soldier's body from 15 to 45 degrees from horizontal.
- From the starting position, perform a controlled Push-Up by maintaining the suspended hand position while flexing the elbows to lower the body toward the ground.
- From the down position, fully extend the elbows to return to the starting position.
- Repeat this exercise 5–10 times.

Figure 10-1. ST1.1 Suspension Push-Up

2. INCLINE CALF RAISE

10-4. The Incline Calf Raise is the second exercise in Suspension Training Drill 1. This exercise uses the suspension trainer to incline the body to increase the challenges to the muscles of the lower leg. Incline exercises position the body in a forward lean. Figure 10-2 breaks down the exercise as an individual Soldier conducts it:

- The starting position for the Incline Calf Raise is the Straddle Stance position with hands holding the straps without tension at waist height.
- From the starting position, lean forward generating tension in the straps, keeping the body in a straight line from the head to the heels. Body weight is supported on the hands and feet. The angle of the body in relation to the ground will be adjusted to meet the goal of the physical training session.
- While maintaining this position, raise the heels up off the ground to balance on the balls of the feet.
- Pause in the up position before lowering the heels back to the ground. Repeat this exercise 5–10 times.

Figure 10-2. ST1.2 Incline Calf Raise

10-5. As skill improves, modify this exercise by—
- Changing the angle of the body in relation to the ground.
- Balancing on one foot and raising one heel at a time.
- Slightly flexing the knees while raising the heels.

3. DECLINE I-T-Y RAISE

10-6. The Decline I-T-Y Raise is the third exercise in Suspension Training Drill 1. This exercise uses the suspension trainer to decline the body to increase the challenges to the muscles of the upper back and shoulders. Decline exercises position the body in a backward lean. Figure 10-3 breaks down the exercise as an individual Soldier conducts it:

- The starting position for the Decline I-T-Y Raise is the Straddle Stance in a backward lean with the suspension straps held at tension above the head.
- From the starting position, pull tension on the straps to move the body to the vertical, creating a straight line when viewed from the side from the hands to the heels. Body weight will be supported by the hands and feet.
- From this position, allow the body to decline further back. As the body moves back, the arms move forward in front of the head. This completes one repetition.
- Complete this pattern for 5–10 repetitions before repeating the exercise with the arms in the "Y" or "T" position. The T position is illustrated in the bottom row of images.

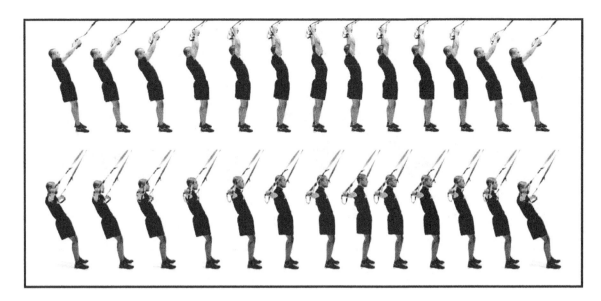

Figure 10-3. ST1.3 Decline I-T-Y Raise

4. ASSISTED SQUAT

10-7. The Assisted Squat is the fourth exercise in Suspension Training Drill 1. This exercise uses the suspension trainer to assist a Soldier's balance and increase the depth of the squat. Figure 10-4 breaks down the exercise as an individual Soldier conducts it:

- The starting position for the Assisted Squat is the Straddle Stance with the suspension straps held at tension at chest height.
- From the starting position, perform a squat, pulling more tension on the straps to assist with balance, depth of the squat motion, or to alleviate the load on the thigh muscles.
- Complete this exercise 5–10 times.

Figure 10-4. ST1.4 Assisted Squat

5. DECLINE BICEPS CURL

10-8. The Decline Biceps Curl is the fifth exercise in Suspension Training Drill 1. This exercise uses the suspension trainer to decline the body to increase the challenges to the biceps muscles using body weight. Decline exercises utilize a backward lean. Figure 10-5 on page 10-4 breaks down the exercise as an individual Soldier conducts it:

- The starting position for the Decline Biceps Curl is the Straddle Stance position with the suspension straps held at tension at chest level using a closed, supinated, or underhand grip.
- From the starting position, lean back either by moving the feet further beneath the strap handles or extending the elbows.
- From the declined position, pull up on the straps by bending the elbows to bring the strap handles toward the chest. The body remains straight throughout the movement.

- Complete this exercise 5–10 times, returning to the starting position after the final repetition.
- To increase the workload or challenge, lengthen the straps to increase the angle of the decline.

Figure 10-5. ST1.5 Decline Biceps Curl

SUSPENSION TRAINING DRILL 2 (ST2)

10-9. Suspension Training Drill 2 (known as ST2) consists of exercises that, like Suspension Training Drill 1, are designed to improve balance and core stability while increasing movement and mobility. Suspension Training Drill 2 exercises require increased levels of strength and mobility. The five Suspension Training Drill 2 exercises are the Assisted Lateral Lunge, Suspension Leg-Tuck and Pike, Decline Pull-Up, Suspension Hamstring Curl, and Assisted Single-Leg Squat. This section also illustrates suspended Climbing Drills 1 and 2 for Soldiers who have access to suspension trainers but lack climbing bar apparatus.

1. ASSISTED LATERAL LUNGE

10-10. The Assisted Lateral Lunge is the first exercise in Suspension Training Drill 2. This exercise uses the suspension trainer to assist a Soldier's balance and increase the range of the lateral lunge movement. Figure 10-6 breaks down the exercise as an individual Soldier conducts it:

- The starting position for the Assisted Lateral Lunge is the Straddle Stance with the suspension straps held at tension at chest height.
- From the starting position, perform an exaggerated step to the left, bending the left knee while pulling increased tension on the straps. The trunk remains facing ahead and, with the right foot remaining in its starting position, the right leg is abducted straight out to the side.
- From this position, pull on the straps to assist with a return to the starting position.
- The lateral lunge movement is then repeated to the right side.
- Complete this exercise 5–10 times.
- The movement can be modified by changing the range of motion of the lunge or the length of the straps.

Figure 10-6. ST2.1 Assisted Lateral Lunge

2. SUSPENSION LEG-TUCK AND PIKE

10-11. The Suspension Leg-Tuck and Pike is the second exercise in Suspension Training Drill 2. It challenges shoulder stability and core strength by suspending the feet above the ground while moving into a prone Leg-Tuck and Pike position. Figure 10-7 breaks down the exercise as a Soldier conducts it:

- The starting position for the Suspension Leg-Tuck and Pike is the Front Leaning Rest position with feet in the straps suspended from the ground. Fully extend elbows, palms flat on the ground. The Soldier adjusts the straps so that his or her body is parallel to the ground.
- Perform a controlled leg tuck, bringing the knees toward the elbows.
- After a brief pause, return to the starting position.
- The next movement is into the Pike position. From the starting position, keeping the knees close together and straight, bring the feet toward the arms.
- Pause in the Pike position before returning to the starting position.
- Complete this exercise 5–10 times.

Figure 10-7. ST2.2 Suspension Leg-Tuck and Pike

3. DECLINE PULL-UP

10-12.   The Decline Pull-Up is the third exercise in Suspension Training Drill. This exercise uses the suspension trainer to decline the body to increase the challenges to the shoulder and arm muscles using body weight. Decline exercises use a backward lean. Figure 10-8 shows the exercise as a Soldier conducts it:

- The starting position for the Decline Pull-Up is the Straddle Stance position with the suspension straps held at tension at chest level using a closed, pronated overhand grip.
- From the starting position, lean back either by moving the feet further beneath the strap handles or extending the elbows.
- From the declined position, pull back up on the straps by bending the elbows to bring the strap handles level with the outside edge of the shoulders. The body remains straight throughout the movement.
- To increase the workload or challenge, lengthen the straps to increase the angle of the decline.

Figure 10-8. ST2.3 Decline Pull-Up

4. SUSPENSION HAMSTRING CURL

10-13.   The Suspension Hamstring Curl is the fourth exercise in Suspension Training Drill 2. It challenges the muscles in the back of the leg used in running, lifting, and jumping. Figure 10-9 breaks down the exercise as a Soldier conducts it:

- The starting position for the Suspension Hamstring Curl is the Supine position with arms on the ground at 45 degrees from the body, knees and hips flexed to 90 degrees with the feet suspended in the strap handles. Shoulders, arms, and trunk rest on the ground. The head may rest on the ground.
- From the starting position, lift the pelvis from the ground to form a straight line from the knees through the hips to the shoulders.
- From this position, straighten the knees until a moderate challenge is felt in the hamstring muscles in the back of the thighs. The pelvis and trunk will remain in the same position.
- After a brief pause, bend the knees, pulling the feet toward the buttocks.
- Repeat this extension and flexion of the knees 5–10 times before returning to the starting position.
- As skill and endurance improves, a modified version of this exercise can be performed by holding in either bent- or straight-knee positions for up to 20–30 seconds.

Figure 10-9. ST2.4 Suspension Hamstring Curl

5. ASSISTED SINGLE LEG SQUAT

10-14.   The Assisted Single Leg Squat is the fifth exercise in Suspension Training Drill 2. This exercise uses the suspension trainer to assist a Soldier's balance and increase the depth of the squat using one leg. This exercise uses the straps pulled into an over-shortened or 'dog-ear' position. Figure 10-10 on page 10-8 breaks down the exercise as a Soldier conducts it:

- The starting position for the Assisted Single Leg Squat is the Straddle Stance with the suspension straps held at tension at chest height.
- From the starting position, raise the right leg to perform a squat on the left leg.
- By increasing more tension on the straps, the suspension trainer assists with balance, assists with depth of the squat motion, or alleviates the load on the thigh muscles.
- Complete this exercise 5 times on the left leg before switching to the right leg.

Figure 10-10. ST2.5 Assisted Single-Leg Squat

10-15. Figure 10-11 illustrates a modified version of the Assisted Single-Leg Squat that positions the elevated foot and leg to the rear.

Figure 10-11. ST2.5a Assisted Single-Leg Squat with alternative movement

6. SUSPENDED CLIMBING DRILLS 1 AND 2

10-16. Soldiers who have access to suspension trainers but lack climbing bar apparatus can conduct suspended Climbing Drills 1 and 2. In this case, Soldiers may modify Climbing Drills 1 and 2 (see paragraphs 6-3 through 6-13) to be performed on the Suspension System. Figure 10-12, figure 10-13, figure 10-14, figure 10-15, figure 10-16 on page 10-10, and figure 10-17 on page 10-10 demonstrate the suspension versions of each of the six Climbing Drill exercises.

Figure 10-12. ST2.6 Suspended Straight-Arm Pull

Figure 10-13. ST2.6 Suspended Heel Hook

Figure 10-14. ST2.6. Suspended Leg Tuck

Figure 10-15. ST2.6 Suspended Pull-Up

Figure 10-16. ST2.6 Suspended Alternating Grip Pull-Up

Figure 10-17. ST2.6 Suspended Flexed Arm Hang

Chapter 11

Landmine Drills

LANDMINE DRILL 1 (LM1)

11-1. Landmine Drills are a series of exercises using a free-weight training device called a landmine. This equipment builds a Soldier's strength in multiple areas of the body and in multiple planes of motion. Landmine exercises, when conducted with the correct intensity and frequency, provide a moderate muscular strength challenge to supplement other physical training free weight exercises. Landmine Drills prepare the body for more vigorous physical training and test events. The alternating, underhand, and overhand grips are used for landmine exercises. All of these grips are closed grips. In some instances, the grip has to be adjusted during the movement and more than one grip may be required.

11-2. Demonstration videos of Landmine Drills are located on the Central Army Registry website at https://atiam.train.army.mil/catalog/search?current=true&filetype=mp4&respect_date=5%2F1%2F2020&search_terms=CIMT. (Copy and paste this address after accessing the Central Army Registry website if the demonstrations do not populate.) Additional support for H2F test events and exercises are located on the Army Combat Fitness Test website at https://www.army.mil/acft/https://www.army.mil/acft/.

1. STRAIGHT-LEG DEADLIFT

11-3. The Straight-Leg Deadlift is the first exercise in Landmine Drill 1 (known as LM1). It strengthens the back of the body—the muscles that form the so-called "posterior chain." Figure 11-1 on page 11-2 breaks down a 4-count version of the exercise as a Soldier conducts it:

- The starting position for the Straight-Leg Deadlift is the Straddle Stance position with the landmine resting on the ground in front of the Soldier's feet.
- On count 1, squat down to grasp the landmine in both hands.
- From the squat position, while keeping the arms straight and extending the knees, hips, and back, lift the landmine from the ground.
- On count 2, while keeping the knees straight, but not locked, bend at the waist to lower the landmine toward the ground. The Soldier's back and arms will remain straight.
- Pause before the landmine reaches the ground. This will be at the point when tension is felt in the back of the thighs.
- To modify the movement and make it easier, place the landmine on the ground to end count 2.
- On count 3, return to the same "up" position performed at the end of count 1.
- On count 4, repeat count 2.
- Complete this exercise 5 times from each side of the bar.

Figure 11-1. LM1.1 Straight-Leg Deadlift

2. DIAGONAL PRESS

11-4. The Diagonal Press is the second exercise in Landmine Drill 1. The movement challenges upper and lower body pull and push strength and coordination. It supports more vigorous testing and combat tasks. Figure 11-2 breaks down a 2-count version of the exercise as a Soldier conducts it:

- The starting position for the Diagonal Press is the Squat position with the landmine resting on the ground. The left side of the body faces the anchor point for the landmine.
- The left hand grips the bar using a closed overhand grip. The right hand grips the bar using a closed underhand grip.
- On count 1, lift the landmine from the ground while simultaneously moving to a Straddle Stance position.
- Move the bar up and out above the left shoulder, pivoting on the left foot to allow the trunk, hips, and right foot to rotate to the left, following the arm and shoulder movement.
- On count 2, return to the starting position, replacing the landmine on the ground to complete one repetition.
- Complete this exercise 5 times on the left side before switching to the right to complete 5 more repetitions.

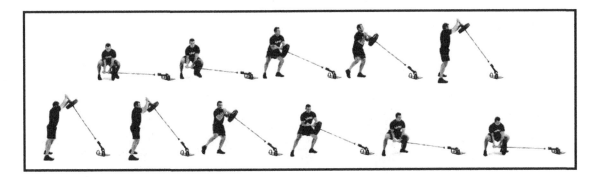

Figure 11-2. LM1.2 Diagonal Press

3. REAR LUNGE

11-5. The Rear Lunge is the third exercise in Landmine Drill 1. It challenges the hip stability and balance as well as prepares Soldiers to move under load from standing to kneeling firing positions. Figure 11-3 breaks down a 4-count version of the exercise as a Soldier conducts it:

- The starting position for the Rear Lunge is the Straddle Stance position with the landmine held at chest height.
- On count 1, take an exaggerated step back with the left leg. The foot will be far enough back to prevent the heel from being on the ground.
- The landmine will continue to be held in front of the chest.
- On count 2, return to the starting position.
- On count 3, repeat the lunging motion with the right leg.
- On Count 4, return to the starting position. This completes one repetition of the exercise.
- Complete this exercise 5–10 times.

Figure 11-3. LM1.3 Rear Lunge

4. 180-DEGREE LANDMINE

11-6. The 180-Degree Landmine is the fourth exercise in Landmine Drill 1. It challenges the arm, shoulder, and core strength and stability in the transverse (dividing top and bottom) and frontal planes. Figure 11-4 on page 11-4 breaks down a 4-count version of the exercise as a Soldier conducts it:

- The starting position for the 180-Degree Landmine is the Straddle Stance position with the landmine held in both hands in front of the right shoulder.
- On count 1, move the bar from the right side of the body up and across to the left side.
- The trunk may follow the shoulder and arm rotation, or remain in place depending on the goal of the physical training session.
- The foot position adjusts as necessary to complete the exercise.

- On count 2, move the landmine from the left back to the right.
- On count 3, repeat count 1.
- On count 4, repeat count 2 to return to the starting position. This completes one repetition of the exercise.
- Repeat this exercise 5–10 times.

Figure 11-4. LM1.4 180-Degree Landmine

5. LATERAL LUNGE

11-7. The Lateral Lunge is the fifth exercise in Landmine Drill 1. It challenges hip strength and mobility in the frontal plane. Figure 11-5 breaks down a 4-count version of the exercise as a Soldier conducts it:
- The starting position for the Lateral Lunge is the Straddle Stance position with the landmine held at waist height.
- On count 1, perform an exaggerated step to the left, bending the left knee while controlling the landmine between waist and chest height.
- The trunk remains facing ahead. The right foot remains in its starting position. The right leg is abducted straight out to the side.
- On count 2, return to the starting position.
- On count 3, repeat the lateral lunge movement to the right.
- On count 4, return to the starting position. This completes one repetition of the exercise.
- Repeat this exercise 5–10 times.

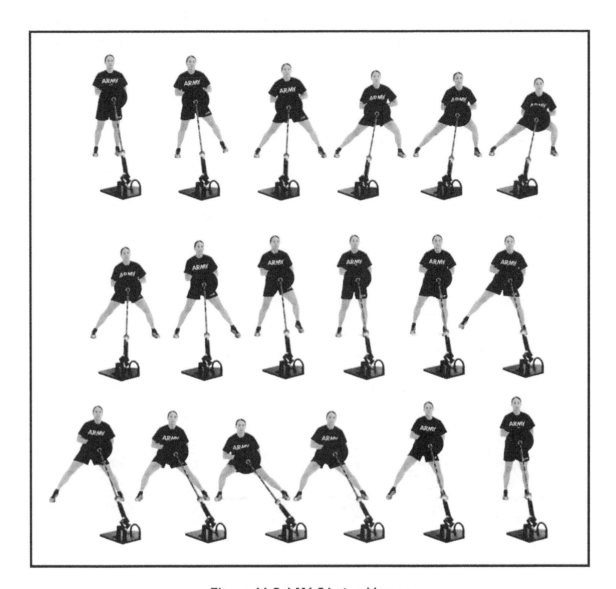

Figure 11-5. LM1.5 Lateral Lunge

LANDMINE DRILL 2 (LM2)

11-8. Landmine Drill 2 (known as LM2) is a more advanced and therefore intense set of exercises using the landmine system. The drill develops a Soldier's strength in multiple areas of the body and in multiple planes of motion to improve muscular strength. It prepares the Soldier for intense physical training and higher levels of performance on test events.

1. DIAGONAL LIFT TO PRESS

11-9. The Diagonal Lift to Press is the first exercise in Landmine Drill 2. It challenges shoulder strength and coordination in both the frontal and sagittal (dividing left and right) planes. Figure 11-6 breaks down a 4-count version of the exercise as a Soldier conducts it:

- The starting position for the Diagonal Lift to Press is the Straddle Stance position with the landmine held in both hands at chest height.
- On count 1, step forward and to the left with the left foot while simultaneously lifting the landmine up and out to the left—a diagonal press.
- The right foot remains in the starting position.
- The trunk may follow the shoulder and arm rotation, or remain in place depending on the goal of the physical training session.
- On count 2, return to the starting position.
- On count 3, repeat the lift and diagonal press motion to the right.
- On count 4, return to the starting position. This completes one repetition of the exercise.
- Complete this exercise 5–10 times.

Figure 11-6. LM2.1 Diagonal Lift to Press

2. SINGLE-ARM CHEST PRESS

11-10. The Single-Arm Chest Press is the second exercise in Landmine Drill 2. It challenges shoulder strength and can be used by injured Soldiers to maintain strength in their non-injured arms. Figure 11-7 breaks down the exercise as a Soldier conducts it:

- The starting position for the Single-Arm Chest Press is the Supine position with knees bent to 90 degrees, head and feet resting on the ground.
- Position the end of the landmine bar above the Soldier's left or right upper arm.
- Grasp the bar with the left or right hand, raising the landmine slightly off the ground if necessary.
- From the starting position, push the landmine up and out from the body. After pausing in the up position, return the weight toward the ground until the upper arm rests on the ground.
- Complete 5–10 repetitions on one side before switching to the other.

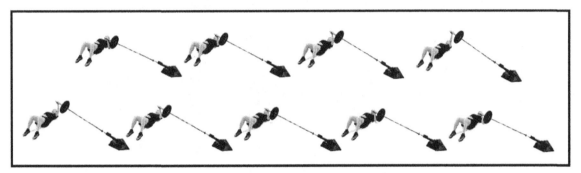

Figure 11-7. LM2.2 Single-Arm Chest Press

3. 180-DEGREE LANDMINE KNEELING

11-11. The 180-Degree Landmine Kneeling is the third exercise in Landmine Drill 2. It strengthens the shoulder and core muscles in the transverse plane as they support movement of the landmine across the body. Figure 11-8 on page 11-8 breaks down a 4-count version of the exercise as a Soldier conducts it:

- The starting position for the 180-Degree Landmine Kneeling is the Kneeling or Half-Kneeling position with both hands holding the landmine in front of the chest.
- On count 1, move the landmine to the left, rotating the trunk to match the movement of the weight.
- On count 2, return to the starting position.
- On count 3, repeat the rotational motion to the right.
- On count 4, return to the starting position. This completes one repetition of the exercise.
- Complete this exercise 5–10 times.

Figure 11-8. LM2.3 180-Degree Landmine Kneeling

4. BENT-OVER ROW

11-12.   The Bent-Over Row is the fourth exercise in Landmine Drill 2. It strengthens muscles in the back of the arms, shoulders, low back, hips, and thighs. Figure 11-9 breaks down a 4-count version of the exercise as a Soldier conducts it:

- The starting position for the Bent-Over Row is the Forward Leaning Stance position with the landmine held with both hands in front of the thighs.
- On count 1, pull the landmine toward the chest with both arms and pause.
- On count 2, return to the starting position.
- On count 3, repeat the rowing motion.
- On count 4, return to the starting position. This completes one repetition of the exercise.
- Complete this exercise 5 times on the left side before switching to the right to complete five more repetitions.

Figure 11-9. LM2.4 Bent-Over Row

5. REAR LUNGE TO PRESS

11-13.   The Rear Lunge to Press is the fifth exercise in Landmine Drill 2. It requires coordination and strength of arm, shoulder, trunk, and leg muscles as they move in the sagittal plane. Figure 11-10 breaks down a 4-count version of the exercise as a Soldier conducts it:

- The starting position for the Rear Lunge to Press is the Straddle Stance position with the landmine held in both hands at chest height.
- On count 1, take an exaggerated step back with the left leg while simultaneously raising the landmine overhead.
- The foot will be far enough back to prevent the heel from being on the ground, and the landmine will be raised so that there is a straight line from the hands through the shoulders, hips, and knees to the rear heel.
- On count 2, return to the starting position.
- On count 3, repeat the lunging motion with the right leg.
- On count 4, return to the starting position. This completes one repetition of the exercise.
- Complete this exercise 5–10 times.

Figure 11-10. LM2.5 Rear Lunge to Press

This page intentionally left blank.

Chapter 12

Pregnancy and Postpartum Physical Training Drills

PREGNANCY AND POSTPARTUM PHYSICAL TRAINING

12-1. Pregnancy and Postpartum Physical Training (known as P3T) programs enable Soldiers to maintain their physical health and fitness through the three trimesters of pregnancy and postpartum period. To maintain readiness, Soldiers exercise three to five times per week for 60–90 minutes per session. Exercise sessions should follow the same principles outlined in this publication but with modifications to accommodate the changes in the pregnant Soldier's fitness and fatigue levels, directives from medical providers, and the Soldier's motivation to train. Otherwise-healthy, postpartum Soldiers may resume core strengthening exercises within a short period after giving birth. Modifications to core and hip strengthening exercises may be necessary at first, but as Soldiers progress, standard movements become easier to execute safely.

12-2. The six exercises in the Pregnancy and Postpartum Physical Training Drill are specific for pregnant and postpartum Soldiers. Paragraphs 12-3 through 12-10 list them for easy reference. The Army Combat Fitness Test website at https://www.army.mil/acft/ has more support for H2F test events and exercises. See demonstration videos for Pregnancy and Postpartum Physical Training Drill exercises at https://atiam.train.army.mil/catalog/search?current=true&filetype=mp4&respect_date=5%2F1%2F2020&search_terms=CIMT—the Central Army Registry website. (Copy and paste this address after accessing the Central Army Registry website if the demonstrations do not populate.)

1. REVERSE SIT-UP

12-3. The Reverse Sit-Up is a modification of the Sit-Up specifically for pregnant or postpartum Soldiers. This exercise safely challenges the abdominal muscles. It can be practiced during the second and third trimesters and in the initial postpartum period. Figure 12-1 on page 12-2 illustrates a breakdown of the exercise a Soldier moving at her own pace conducts it:

- The starting position is Sitting position with knees bent, feet on the floor, and hands and forearms crossed over the front of the abdomen and pulling the sides inward. This creates support to reduce the work of the abdominal muscles.
- From the starting position, lower the trunk as far as comfortable toward the ground while keeping the feet on the ground throughout the movement.
- Return to the sitting position.
- Progress to lower drops as skill improves, keeping feet on the ground throughout the movement.
- Repeat this exercise up to 10 times.

Figure 12-1. P3T1 Reverse Sit-Up

2. OBLIQUE SIT-UP

12-4. The Oblique Sit-Up is a modification of the Sit-Up specifically for pregnant or postpartum Soldiers. This exercise safely challenges the oblique muscles of the abdomen. It can be practiced during the first trimester and postpartum period by Soldiers who have no rectus diastasis or no diastasis wider than two fingers. Figure 12-2 shows a breakdown of the exercise as a Soldier moving at her own pace conducts it:

- The starting position is the Supine position with knees bent, and feet, trunk, and head on the floor. Fingers are locked together behind the head.
- From the starting position, cross the right leg over the left knee before raising the head and left shoulder and arm up toward the right knee.
- If necessary, keep the right shoulder and upper arm on the ground to support the movement. Pause before lowering back the starting position.
- Repeat this exercise up to 10 times before performing the same movement on the opposite side.

Figure 12-2. P3T2 Oblique Sit-Up

3. MODIFIED SIT-UP

12-5. The Modified Sit-Up is a modification of the Sit-Up specifically for pregnant or postpartum Soldiers. This exercise safely challenges the muscles of the abdomen. It can be practiced through the first trimester and postpartum period by all Soldiers who have no rectus diastasis or no diastasis wider than two fingers. Figures 12-3 and 12-4 show a breakdown of the exercise as a Soldier moving at her own pace conducts it:

- The starting position is the Supine position with knees bent, feet, trunk and head on the floor. Arms are crossed over the abdomen with hands holding the sides to splint the abdominal muscles.
- From the starting position, lift the head, shoulders, and chest toward the thighs while continuing to splint the abdomen.
- Pause before lowering back to the starting position.
- Reduce the difficulty of the exercise by only lifting the head or just the shoulders from the ground
- Repeat this exercise up to 10 times.

Figure 12-3. P3T3 Modified Sit-Up

Figure 12-4. P3T3 Modified Sit-Up—head lift

4. STANDING TRUNK CURVE

12-6. The Standing Trunk Curve is an exercise specifically for pregnant or postpartum Soldiers. This exercise safely challenges control of the muscles of the abdomen and pelvis. It can be practiced through the third trimester and postpartum period by all Soldiers. Figure 12-5 and figure 12-6 show a breakdown of the exercise as a Soldier moving at her own pace conducts it:

- The starting position is the Straddle stance position with hands on hips.
- From the starting position, raise the arms up and out from the shoulders at 45 degrees while taking a deep breath in. Simultaneously draw the waistline in and up. Exhale but hold the curve in the abdomen created by this procedure.
- Relax and return to the starting position.

12-7. To modify the Standing Trunk Curve—

- Increase difficulty by taking a second inhalation, drawing the abdomen further in and staying tall in the spine and upper chest.
- Decrease difficulty by performing it in a Sitting position with hands on knees and elbows out.
- Take a few normal breaths between repetitions.
- Repeat this exercise up to 10 times at own pace.

Figure 12-5. P3T4 Standing Trunk Curve

Figure 12-6. P3T4 Seated Trunk Curve

5. DEEP SUMO SQUAT

12-8. The Deep Sumo Squat is an exercise specifically for pregnant or postpartum Soldiers (see figure 12-7, figure 12-8, and figure 12-9). This exercise safely helps to prepare Soldiers for delivery of their babies. It challenges balance and hip mobility and prepares for a return to similar movements with free weights in the postpartum and reconditioning periods after pregnancy. The standing version of this exercise should not be performed until pelvic floor muscles have regained their strength after pregnancy. The Soldier conducts the exercise moving at her own pace with the following movements:

- The starting position is the Sitting position with hands on the ground at the sides.
- From the starting position, bend the knees to draw both feet up to either the left or right side of the body.
- Move both hands to the ground.
- Use the arms to support the movement into a squat with the feet and knees turned out to open the pelvic floor.
- Support the position with hands on the ground, elbows between the knees.
- Relax in this position for 30–60 seconds or to tolerance before return to the starting position.
- To modify the Deep Sumo Squat, hold a small weight (kettlebell or dumbbell) in front of the body to assist with balance
- Repeat 2–3 times at own pace.

Figure 12-7. P3T5 Deep Sumo Squat

Figure 12-8. P3T5 Deep Sumo Squat—weight-assisted

12-9. Increase the level of difficulty by moving to the Deep Sumo Squat from the standing position without placing the hands on the ground.

Figure 12-9. P3T5 Deep Sumo Squat—from Standing position without weight

6. PELVIC CLOCK

12-10.   The Pelvic Clock is an exercise specifically for pregnant or postpartum Soldiers. This exercise safely challenges the Soldier's muscular control and the mobility of her pelvis and lumbo-sacral region. It can be practiced through the third trimester and postpartum period. Figure 12-10 shows the exercise as a Soldier moving at her own pace conducts it:

- The starting position is the Supine position with knees bent, feet, trunk and head on the floor. Hands are placed on the bony prominences on the front of the pelvis below the waistline.
- It may help the Soldier to imagine a clock resting on the front of the pelvis. 12 is toward the head.
- From the starting position, flatten the low back against the ground. The hands will move down to the ground. Consider this as movement "toward 12 o'clock." Hold for 5 seconds.
- From this position, move back through the starting position to rotate the pelvis up—"movement toward 6 o'clock." Hold for 5 seconds.
- As skill improves, move to other positions on the clock—left side up as right side of the pelvis moves down is "movement to 3 o'clock."
- "Movement to 9 o'clock" is created by tilting the pelvis up on the right and down on the left.
- Pause for 5 seconds in each position before moving around the clock.
- If the Soldier moves around the 12 positions on the clock, it would take one minute to complete.

Figure 12-10. P3T6 Pelvic Clock

Chapter 13

Strength Training Circuit

STRENGTH TRAINING

13-1. The Strength Training Circuit (known as STC) consists of ten sequenced exercise stations using strength training equipment and climbing exercises performed for a designated time until all exercises have been completed. Movement and distance between stations may be varied and may include exercises from Military Movement and Running Drills. This is a total body resistance circuit that promotes muscular endurance. The amount of weight and the length of rest intervals can be increased or decreased to target other components of physical fitness.

13-2. Videos of the Strength Training Circuit located on the Central Army Registry website at https://atiam.train.army.mil/catalog/search?current=true&filetype=mp4&respect_date=5%2F1%2F2020&search_terms=CIMT demonstrate movements. (Copy and paste this address after accessing the Central Army Registry website if the demonstrations do not populate.) Additional support for H2F test events and exercises are located on the Army Combat Fitness Test website at https://www.army.mil/acft/.

1. SUMO SQUAT

13-3. The Sumo Squat is the first exercise in the Strength Training Circuit. The starting position for the Sumo Squat is the Straddle Stance position with the feet slightly wider than the shoulders and the toes pointing outward. Hold a single kettlebell with both hands in front of the body, palms pronated to face the body. Figure 13-1 on page 13-2 shows the exercise as a Soldier conducts it for one minute at station 1 of the Strength Training Circuit. The cadence is always slow:

- On count 1, squat while leaning slightly forward from the waist with the head up. Move downward until the upper legs are parallel to the ground.
- On count 2, reverse the movement performed in count 1 to return to the starting position.
- On count 3, repeat count 1.
- On count 4, return to the starting position.
- Complete one minute of repetitions, stopping to rest if necessary, or adjusting the weight and range of movement to match the required performance.

Figure 13-1. STC1 Sumo Squat

2. STRAIGHT-LEG DEADLIFT

13-4. The Straight-Leg Deadlift is the second exercise in the Strength Training Circuit (see figure 13-2). A Soldier conducts the exercise for one minute at station 2 of the Strength Training Circuit. The cadence is always slow:

- The starting position for the Straight-Leg Deadlift is the Straddle Stance position. Hold the kettlebells in front of the legs using a pronated grip. Keep the knees slightly flexed—not locked—and in the same flexed position throughout the exercise.
- On count 1, flex forward from the waist, keeping the head in line with the spine to avoid extending the neck. While keeping the back straight, move down until the back is parallel to the ground. Slightly adjust knee flexion to increase the engagement of the hamstring muscles in the back of the thigh.
- On count 2, reverse the movement performed in count 1 to return to the starting position.
- On count 3, repeat count 1.
- Complete one minute of repetitions, stopping to rest if necessary, or adjusting the weight and range of movement to match the required performance.

Figure 13-2. STC2 Straight-Leg Deadlift

3. FORWARD LUNGE

13-5. The Forward Lunge is the third exercise in the Strength Training Circuit. Figure 13-3 on page 13-4 breaks down the exercise a Soldier conducts it for one minute at station 3 of the Strength Training Circuit:

- The starting position for the Forward Lunge is the Straddle Stance position. Hold the kettlebells at the sides using a neutral grip.
- On count 1, step forward with the left leg as in the Forward Lunge, allowing the left knee to bend until the left thigh is parallel to the ground. Lean slightly forward from the waist and bring the kettlebells to the left and right sides of the forward leg.
- On count 2, reverse the movement performed in count 1 to return to the starting position.
- On count 3, repeat count 1, stepping forward with the right leg.
- On count 4, return to the starting position.
- Complete one minute of repetitions, stopping to rest if necessary, or adjusting the weight and range of movement to match the required performance.
- Complete one minute of repetitions, stopping to rest if necessary, or adjusting the weight and range of movement to match the required performance.

Figure 13-3. STC3 Forward Lunge

4. 8-COUNT STEP-UP

13-6. The 8-Count Step-Up is the fourth exercise in the Strength Training Circuit. Figure 13-4 shows the exercise as a Soldier conducts it for one minute at station 1 of the Strength Training Circuit:

- The starting position for the 8-Count Step-Up is the Straddle Stance position. Hold the kettlebells at the sides with a neutral grip.
- On count 1, step up on to a 12- to 18-inch step with the left foot, keeping the kettlebells at the sides of the body.
- On count 2, step up with the right foot.
- On count 3, step down with the left foot.
- On count 4, step down with the right foot.
- On count 5, step up with the right foot, keeping the kettlebells at the sides of the body.
- On count 6, step up with the left foot,

- On count 7, step down with the right foot.
- On count 8, step down with the left foot.
- Complete one minute of repetitions, stopping to rest if necessary, or adjusting the weight and range of movement to match the required performance.

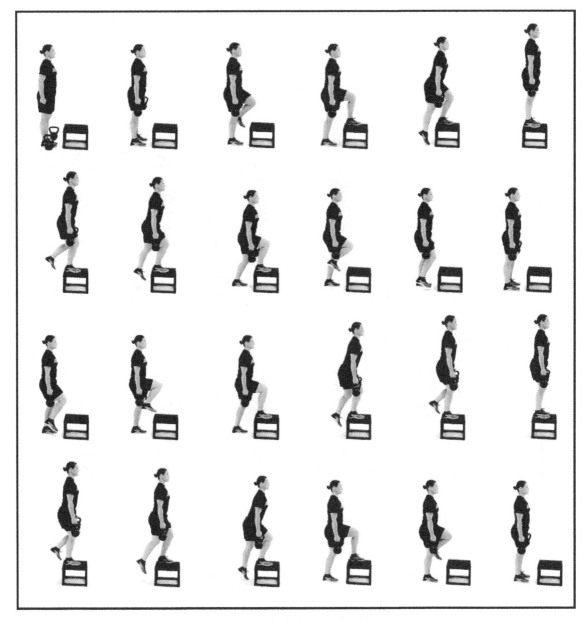

Figure 13-4. STC4 8-Count Step-up

5A. PULL-UP

13-7. The Pull-Up is the fifth exercise in the strength training circuit. This exercise develops the Soldier's ability to climb without using the legs. Figure 13-5 breaks down the exercise as a Soldier conducts it in the Strength Training Circuit for up to one minute:

- The starting position for the Pull-Up is the Straight-Arm Hang using the closed overhand grip.
- After repeating 5 times, dismount to the Straddle Stance position on the ground.
- On the command, "GO," flex the elbows, raising the body in a straight line until the head is above the bar.
- If the Soldier cannot complete one minute of pull-ups, he or she will perform the Straight-Arm Pull.

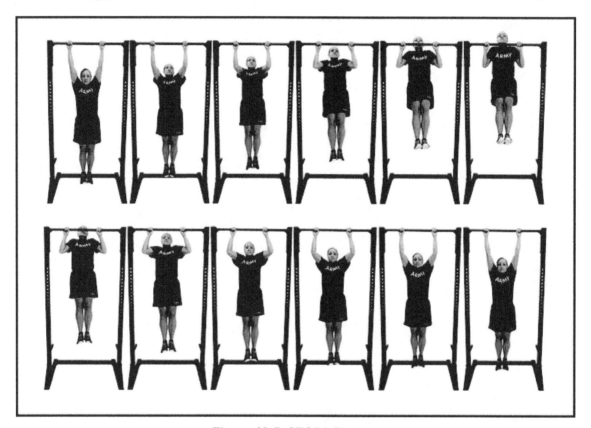

Figure 13-5. STC5A Pull-up

5B: STRAIGHT-ARM PULL

13-8. The Straight-Arm Pull is the alternate fifth exercise in the Strength Training Circuit. This exercise develops the Soldier's ability to pull up without using the legs. Figure 13-6 shows the exercise as it would be conducted by an individual Soldier during the Strength Training Circuit:

- The starting position for the Straight Arm Pull is the Straight-Arm Hang using the closed overhand grip.
- After repeating 5 times, dismount to the Straddle Stance position on the ground.
- On count 1, from the starting position and keeping the arms straight, pull the body up using a shrugging motion.
- Repeat the exercise for up to one minute.

Figure 13-6. STC5B Straight-Arm Pull

6. SUPINE CHEST PRESS

13-9. The Supine Chest Press is the sixth exercise in the Strength Training Circuit. This exercise strengthens the chest, shoulder, and triceps muscles. It develops the Soldier's ability to push during more vigorous combatives, testing, and combat tasks. Figure 13-7 illustrates the exercise as a Soldier conducts it for one minute at station 6 of the Strength Training Circuit:

- The starting position for the Supine Chest Press is the Supine position with knees bent to 90 degrees, feet 8–12 inches apart and flat on the ground. The head and upper arms are resting on the ground.
- Holding a kettlebell of the same weight in each hand using a closed partial pronated grip, bend the elbows to allow the kettlebells to rest on the front of the shoulders.
- On the command, "BEGIN," extend the elbows to raise the kettlebells straight up in front of the shoulders, rotating to a fully pronated grip.
- Return to the starting position.
- Continue the exercise at own pace for one minute. Increase or decrease the kettlebell weight if necessary, continuing only if the Supine Chest Press movement can be completed to standard.

Figure 13-7. STC6 Supine Chest Press

7. BENT-OVER ROW

13-10. The Bent-Over Row is the seventh exercise in the Strength Training Circuit. This exercise strengthens the muscles of the upper back, the shoulder girdle, and the biceps. Heavier weight also challenges the muscles in the lower back, gluteal region, and hamstrings. Figure 13-8 breaks down the exercise as a Soldier conducts it for one minute at station 7 of the Strength Training Circuit:

- The starting position for the Bent-Over Row is the Forward Leaning Stance position with arms hanging in front of the legs. Hold kettlebells of equal weight using a closed neutral grip—palms facing each other.
- On the command, "BEGIN," bend the elbows to pull the kettlebells toward the chest. The legs, torso, and head remain in their starting positions.
- Continue the exercise at own pace for one minute. Increase or decrease the kettlebell weight if necessary, continuing only if the exercise can be completed to standard.

Figure 13-8. STC7 Bent-Over Row

8. OVERHEAD PUSH-PRESS

13-11. The Overhead Push-Press is the eighth exercise in the Strength Training Circuit. This exercise strengthens the Soldier's triceps and shoulder muscle endurance. This improves the Soldier's skill in moving heavier weight overhead to build muscular power and strength. Figure 13-9 shows the exercise as a Soldier conducts it for one minute at station 8 of the Strength Training Circuit:

- The starting position for the Overhead Push-Press is the Straddle Stance position. Hold the kettlebells at the collar bones in the rack position, using a closed neutral grip (palms will be facing each other).
- On the command, "BEGIN," slightly flex the hips and knees into a mini-squat before quickly and forcefully extending the elbows to push the weights overhead. At the top of the movement, the kettlebells will be above the shoulders.
- Continue to look straight ahead throughout the movement.
- Slightly flex the hips and knees into a mini-squat before returning the weight to the starting position. This squat helps to absorb the impact of the weight's descent.
- Continue the exercise at own pace for one minute. Increase or decrease the kettlebell weight if necessary, continuing only if the exercise can be completed to standard.

Figure 13-9. STC8 Overhead Push-Press

9. SUPINE BODY TWIST

13-12. The Supine Body Twist is the ninth exercise in the Strength Training Circuit. This exercise strengthens the trunk muscles used for movement in the transverse plane. By keeping the knees together it also strengthens hip adductor muscles often referred to as the groin muscles. Figure 13-10 shows the exercise as a Soldier conducts it for one minute at station 9 of the Strength Training Circuit:

- The starting position for the Supine Body Twist is the Supine position with the hips and knees bent to 90 degrees so that the feet are off the ground. The head is off the ground. One kettlebell is held in front of and off the chest. The kettlebell handle is held by both hands, palms facing each other. The bell portion of the kettlebell is positioned above the stomach, not above the head.
- On the command, "BEGIN," rotate the kettlebell to the left and the legs to the right as far as possible under control. Keep the weight away from the body and the arms and head off the ground.
- Return to the starting position.
- Repeat the first movement—this time to the opposite side—arms to the right and legs to the left.
- The head may turn with the arms but should not lift more than 2–4 inches from the ground.
- Continue the exercise at own pace for one minute maintaining the range of motion. Increase or decrease the kettlebell weight if necessary, continuing only if the exercise can be completed to standard.

Figure 13-10. STC9 Supine Body Twist

10. LEG TUCK

13-13.   The Leg Tuck is the tenth exercise in the Strength Training Circuit. This exercise combines upper body an abdominal strength to develop the Soldier's ability to hang while moving the legs into different support positions for climbing. Figure 13-11 breaks down the exercise as a Soldier conducts it for one minute at station 10 of the Strength Training Circuit:

- The starting position for the Leg Tuck is the Straight-Arm Hang using the closed overhand grip.
- On the command, "BEGIN," flex the elbows and hips, raising the legs until the thighs touch the elbows.
- Return to the starting position.
- Continue the exercise at own pace for one minute. Stop for 3–5 seconds rest if needed, continuing only if the exercise can be completed to standard.
- On the command, "ROTATE," return to the first station in the Strength Training Circuit.

Figure 13-11. STC10 Leg Tuck

Chapter 14

Free Weight Training

FREE WEIGHTS

14-1. Free Weight Training (known as FW) exercises are divided into two groups, core and assistive. Core exercises load multiple regions of the body at the same time and require skill and coordination for proper movement and progression to heavier weight. Once the Soldier masters the core exercise movements, these exercises provide the drive for a Soldier's development of muscle power and strength. Assistive exercises more likely isolate to one or two limbs and load a smaller number or group of muscles. Assistive exercises therefore complement core exercises and can be used to prepare for or recover from core exercises.

14-2. Demonstration videos of Free Weight Training exercises are located on the Army Combat Fitness Test website at https://www.army.mil/acft/ and on the Central Army Registry website at https://atiam.train.army.mil/catalog/search?current=true&filetype=mp4&respect_date=5%2F1%2F2020&search_terms=CIMT. (Copy and paste this address after accessing the Central Army Registry website if the demonstrations do not populate.)

FREE WEIGHT CORE TRAINING EXERCISES

14-3. Free Weight Core training aims to increase the body's muscle strength and endurance. The exercises listed in paragraphs 14-4 through 14-12 use three main types of free weights—straight bar, kettlebells, and dumbbells—to develop muscles in functional groups or regions primarily utilizing lifting, pulling, or pushing motions.

FRONT SQUAT

14-4. The Front Squat is a free-weight exercise performed throughout a Soldier's career to improve lower body muscular strength and endurance. Soldiers use it to improve training and testing performance that supports a wide range of combat and occupational physical tasks. There are a wide range of modifications in position and equipment for the Squat. Figure 14-1 on page 14-2 breaks down the exercise as it would be conducted by an individual Soldier using three types of free weights—straight bar, kettlebells, and dumbbells:

- The starting position for the Front Squat is the Straddle Stance position with the toes pointed slightly outward. The bar is held across the top of the chest just below the collar bones using the crossed arms with pronated grip.
- When performing the Squat with dumbbells or kettlebells, start in the Straddle Stance position with the weight in a similar position to the straight bar—the racked position for the kettlebells or resting on top of the shoulders for the dumbbells.
- From the starting position, bend the knees and slowly lower the body downward until there is a 90-degree angle between the upper and lower leg.
- Return to the starting position.
- Repeat this movement for the correct number of repetitions and sets required to meet the goal of the free weight session.

Figure 14-1. FW1 Front Squat

FRONT SQUAT CAUTION

- Do not round out the upper back.
- The knees stay aligned over the feet and the heels stay on the ground.
- Progress to deeper squat positions as strength improves.
- Always lift a weight that can be controlled throughout the range of motion.

14-5. The Front Squat requires a spotter. The spotter maintains the following:

- Starting position for the spotter is the Straddle Stance position behind the lifter.
- Place hands between the upper arm and waist of the lifter—not touching.

- Assist the lifter as needed in un-racking the weight and moving to the starting position. Once the lifter is ready, position hands close to each side of the lifter's trunk.
- During the squat movement, move with the lifter until the lifter has racked the weight after completing the last repetition.
- Always remains prepared to assist if the lifter becomes unstable.
- Stay especially cautious when the lifter is conducting a power or muscular strength routine when the weight is likely to be heavy.

BACK SQUAT

14-6. The Back Squat is a common variation of the Front Squat. A Back Squat may be performed with the bar across the upper back. When performing the Squat with dumbbells or kettlebells, start in the Straddle Stance position with one weight at each side using a neutral grip. Figure 14-2 demonstrates a Soldier performing the exercise with the following movements:

- The starting position for the Back Squat is the Straddle Stance position with the toes pointed slightly outward. From the starting position, bend the knees and slowly lower the body downward until there is a 90-degree angle between the upper and lower leg.
- Return to the starting position.
- Repeat this movement for the correct number of repetitions and sets required to meet the goal of the free weight session.
- Maintain a natural arch in the lower back with the head and neck staying in alignment to avoid extending the neck. Do not round out the upper back.
- Keep the knees stay aligned over the feet and the heels on the ground.
- Initially do not squat deeper than 90 degrees. Progress to deeper positions as strength improves. Always lift a weight that can be controlled.

Figure 14-2. FW2 Back Squat

14-7. The Back Squat requires a spotter. The spotter maintains the following:

- The starting position for the spotter is the Straddle Stance behind the lifter with hands close to but not touching each side of the body between the waist and the upper arms.
- Assist the lifter as needed in un-racking the weight and moving to the starting position.
- During the squat movement, move with the lifter until the lifter has racked the weight after completing the last repetition.

- Always remains prepared to assist if the lifter becomes unstable. Spot with the hands under the chest.
- Stay especially cautious when the lifter is conducting a power or muscular strength set when the weight is likely to be heavy.

DEADLIFT

14-8. The Deadlift is a Free Weight Core exercise performed throughout a Soldier's career to improve lower body muscular strength and endurance. This lift requires trunk and shoulder stability and strength. It can be used to improve training and testing performance that supports a wide range of combat and occupational physical tasks. There are a wide range of modifications in position and equipment for the Deadlift. Figures 14-3 and 14-4 show the exercise as an individual Soldier conducts it using two of the three types of free weights—straight bar or barbell, kettlebells, and dumbbells:

- The starting position for the Deadlift is the Forward Leaning Stance position. Grasp the barbell below the knees and near the shins with the arms fully extended using a closed overhand or alternating grip.
- When lifting with a hex bar, the bar requires a neutral grip.
- When performing the Deadlift with dumbbells or kettlebells, start in the Forward Leaning Stance position with one weight at each side using a neutral grip.
- From the starting position, extend the hips and knees while keeping the spine straight and arms extended.
- As the barbell lifts from the ground, move the hips forward to meet it.
- Pause in an upright posture before returning the weight to the starting position under control. Do not drop the weight. Throughout the lift, do not let the spine or shoulders round forward.
- Keep knees in line over the feet.
- Repeat this movement for the correct number of repetitions and sets required to meet the goal of the free weight session.

Figure 14-3. FW3 Deadlift—straight bar

Figure 14-4. FW3 Deadlift—kettlebells

14-9. The Straight-Leg Deadlift is a variation of the Deadlift that further challenges the muscles in the lower back, hips, and legs. Figure 14-5 breaks down the exercise as it would be conducted by an individual Soldier using a straight bar and dumbbells:

- The starting position for the Straight-Leg Deadlift using the straight bar is the Straddle Stance position. Hold the bar with a grip suited to the Soldier's capability, the equipment, and the goal of the exercise session. Keep the knees slightly flexed—not locked—and in the same flexed position throughout the exercise.
- From the starting position, flex forward from the waist, keeping the head aligned with the spine to avoid extending the neck.
- While keeping the back straight, bend over until the back is parallel to the ground. Slightly adjust knee flexion to increase the engagement of the hamstring muscles in the back of the thigh.
- After a brief pause, reverse the movement to return to the starting position.
- Always lift a weight that can be controlled throughout the range of motion.
- Use the same movement with different grips for the kettlebell and dumbbell versions of this exercise.
- Repeat this movement for the correct number of repetitions and sets required to meet the goal of the free weight session.

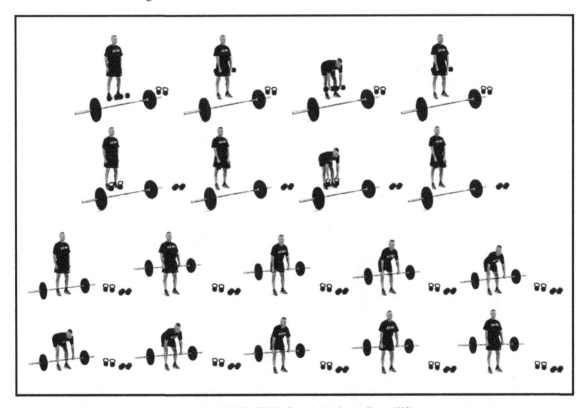

Figure 14-5. FW3 Straight-Leg Deadlift

BENCH PRESS

14-10.   The Bench Press is a free-weight exercise performed throughout a Soldier's career to improve upper body muscular strength and endurance. When conducted with free weights, it requires stability of the trunk, lower back, hips, and upper leg muscles. It can be varied by changing the equipment or angle of the bench. Figures 14-6, 14-7, 14-8, and 14-9 (on page 14-8) show variations of the exercise as a Soldier conducts it:

- The starting position for the Bench Press is the Supine position laying on the bench with feet on the floor. Grasp the weights with hands using a closed pronated grip slightly wider than shoulder width. Shoulders, head, and lower back are firmly against the bench.
- Position the barbell above the upper chest in the rack.
- From the starting position, remove the bar from the supports, placing it over the chest with the elbows fully extended.
- From this position, lower the bar by bending the elbows until the bar is just above the sternum.
- After a brief pause, reverse the movement to return to the up position. The bar should move evenly into the up position—remaining parallel to the ground as it moves up.

BENCH PRESS CAUTIONS

- Do not jerk the weight, shrug, arch the back, or allow the hips to rise off the bench during the exercise.
- Keep feet firmly on the ground to build maximum strength over time.
- As the weight increases, using proper breathing technique on the lift will become more important.
- Inhale on the downward movement and exhale on the upward movement.
- Practice this breathing technique on lighter weight to improve skill later.

Figure 14-6. FW4 Bench Press—straight bar

Figure 14-7. FW4 Bench Press—dumbbell

Figure 14-8. FW4 Bench Press—kettlebell

Figure 14-9. FW4 Bench Press—decline

INCLINE BENCH

14-11. The Incline Bench is a free-weight exercise performed throughout a Soldier's career to improve upper body muscular strength and endurance. This lift requires trunk and shoulder stability and strength. It can be used to improve training and testing performance that supports a wide range of combat and occupational physical tasks. There are a wide range of modifications in position and equipment for the Incline Bench. Soldiers conduct it using three types of free weights—straight bar or barbell, kettlebells, and dumbbells. Figure 14-10 illustrates the exercise as an individual Soldier conducts it using the straight bar:

- The starting position for the Incline Bench is the Supine position on an inclined bench with both feet on the ground and hips, shoulders, and head firmly against the bench. Grasp the barbell with a closed overhand, pronated grip slightly wider than shoulder width. Remove the bar from the supports placing it over the chest with the elbows fully extended.
- From the starting position, bend both elbows to lower the weight to just above the chest.
- Press the weight back to the starting position. Do not jerk or shrug the shoulders, arch the back, or allow the hips to rise off the bench during the movement.
- Repeat this movement for the correct number of repetitions and sets required to meet the goal of the free weight session.

Figure 14-10. FW5 Incline Bench

14-12. The Bench Press and Incline Bench each require a spotting position. The spotter maintains the following:

- The spotter stands at the head of the bench in the Straddle Stance position with feet slightly staggered.
- Grasp the bar with a closed alternating grip in between the lifter's hands. On a signal from the lifter, assist the lifter with moving the bar from the supports to guide it over the lifter's chest.
- Follow the path of the bar by slightly flexing the knees, hips, and trunk while maintaining a flat back. Keep an alternating grip position close to but not touching the bar as it is lowered to the chest.
- Reverse this movement until the lifter signals for an assist with returning the bar to the supports.
- If the lifter becomes unstable or begins to fail to control the weight, immediately assist with completing the lift.

FREE WEIGHT ASSISTIVE TRAINING EXERCISES

14-13. Free Weight Assistive training is designed to increase the muscle strength and endurance of the body's extremities, primarily the arms and legs. The exercises listed in paragraphs 14-15 through 14-26 use three main types of free weights—straight bar, kettlebells, and dumbbells—to develop muscles in the extremities with support from groups of muscles in the core, such as the back or chest muscles.

SUMO DEADLIFT

14-14. The Sumo Deadlift is a free-weight exercise performed throughout a Soldier's career to improve lower body muscular strength and endurance. It is a modification of the Deadlift that further challenges a Soldier's coordination, balance, and hip mobility. Figure 14-11 on page 14-10 illustrates a Soldier performing the exercise using two of the three types of free weights—straight bar, kettlebells, and dumbbells:

- The starting position for the Sumo Deadlift is the Straddle Stance position with feet slightly wider than shoulder width and toes pointing outward. When performing the lift with dumbbells or kettlebells, start in the Straddle Stance position with a single weight held between and in front of the legs. Knees are bent, back is straight, and the bar or weight is held in both hands with a grip suited to the lifter's capability, the equipment, and the goal of the exercise session.
- From the starting position, straighten the knees and slowly raise the trunk into the upright Position of Attention.
- Pause before reversing the upward movement to return to the starting position.
- Maintain a natural arch in the lower back with the head and neck staying in alignment to avoid extending the neck. Do not round out the upper back.
- Keep the knees and feet turned outward throughout the movement. The wider stance permits a lower lifting range of motion.
- Always lift a weight that can be controlled throughout the range of motion.
- Use the same movement with different grips for the kettlebell and dumbbell versions.
- Repeat this movement for the correct number of repetitions and sets required to meet the goal of the free weight session.

Figure 14-11. FW6 Sumo Deadlift

HEEL RAISE

14-15. The Heel Raise is a free-weight exercise performed throughout a Soldier's career to improve lower leg muscular strength and endurance. When conducted with free weights, it requires stability of the trunk, lower back, hips, and upper leg muscles. Figure 14-12 illustrates a Soldier performing the exercise using straight bar, kettlebells, and dumbbells:

- The starting position for the Heel Raise using the straight bar is the Straddle Stance position.
- The knees are straight or slightly flexed depending upon which muscle in the lower leg is being strengthened. Straight for the gastrocnemius and bent for the soleus muscle.
- Hold the barbell across the upper back. The feet may be elevated, so that the heels can be slightly lower than the balls of the feet to achieve a full range of motion. When using dumbbells or kettlebells, hold one at each side using a neutral grip.
- From the starting position, rise up on the balls of the feet.
- After a brief pause, reverse the movement to return to the starting position. Drop the heels as far as possible. Slightly adjust knee flexion to increase the engagement of the targeted lower leg muscle.
- Always lift a weight that can be controlled throughout the range of motion.
- Use same movement with neutral grips for the kettlebell and dumbbell versions of this exercise.
- Repeat this movement for the correct number of repetitions and sets required to meet the goal of the free weight session.

Figure 14-12. FW7 Heel Raise

BENT-OVER ROW

14-16.   The Bent-Over Row is a free-weight exercise performed throughout a Soldier's career to improve upper back strength and endurance. When conducted with free weights, it supports other core exercises like the Deadlift. It can be varied by changing the equipment or by isolating to just one arm. Figure 14-13 on page 14-12 breaks down the exercise as it would be conducted by an individual Soldier using a variety of approaches:

- The starting position for the Bent-Over Row is the Forward Leaning Stance position with arms fully extended down and in front of the body holding the bar with an overhand grip in front of the legs.
- Position the arms slightly wider than shoulder width and keep the head in line with the spine.
- From the starting position, pull the weight toward the chest until the upper arms are parallel to the ground. Elbows should be up and pointing to the rear. Head and spine position remain in the starting position.

- After a brief pause, reverse the movement to return to the down position.
- As the weight and repetitions increase, concentrate on preventing the upper back and shoulders from rounding forward.
- Always lift a weight that can be controlled throughout the range of motion.
- Use the same movement with neutral grips for the kettlebell and dumbbell versions.
- Repeat this movement for the correct number of repetitions and sets required to meet the goal of the free weight session.

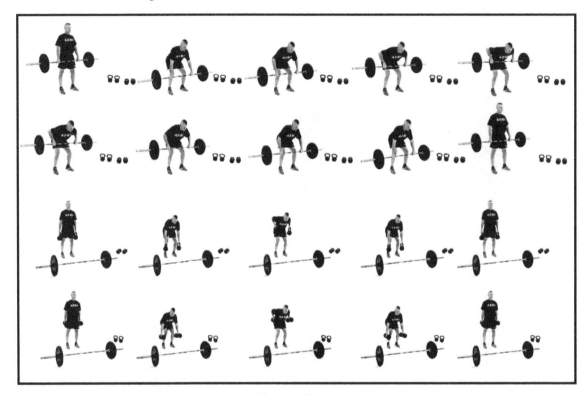

Figure 14-13. FW8 Bent-Over Row

SINGLE-ARM BENT-OVER ROW

14-17.   The Single-Arm Bent-Over Row is a modified version of the Bent-Over Row. It can be performed with a single dumbbell or kettlebell. Figure 14-14 breaks down the exercise as an individual Soldier conducts it using a variety of approaches:

- The starting position for the Single Arm Bent-Over Row requires the use of a bench. The right arm and knee rest on the bench to support the body on that side. The left leg rests on the ground and the left arm is fully extended down and in front of the body holding the dumbbell with an overhand grip.
- The back is straight and the head is in line with the spine.
- From the starting position, pull the weight toward the chest until the upper arm is parallel to the ground. Elbow should be up and pointing to the rear. Head and spine position remain in the starting position.
- Move the dumbbell from the down position to the up position.
- After a brief pause, reverse the movement to return to the down position.
- As the weight and repetitions increase, concentrate on preventing the upper back and shoulder from rounding forward.
- Always lift a weight that can be controlled throughout the range of motion.

- Use the same movement with neutral grips for the kettlebell version of this exercise.
- Repeat this movement for the correct number of repetitions and sets required to meet the goal of the free weight session. Switch to the opposite side to perform the same movement for the right side.

Figure 14-14. FW9 Single-Arm Bent-Over Row

UPRIGHT ROW

14-18.   The Upright Row is a modified version of the Bent-Over Row. It focuses the work on the upper trapezius as well as those muscles targeted in the Bent-Over Row. It can be performed with a straight bar, dumbbells, or kettlebells. Figures 14-15 and 14-16 on page 14-14 illustrate the exercise as it would be conducted by an individual Soldier using a straight bar and kettlebells:

- The starting position for the Upright Row is the Straddle Stance position with arms fully extended and down in front of the body holding the straight bar or kettlebell with a closed overhand grip. A single weight or short bar can be used when first performing this exercise.
- From the starting position, pull the weight up to the collar bones until the arms are parallel to the ground.
- After a brief pause, reverse the movement to return to the down position.
- As the weight and repetitions increase, concentrate on preventing the upper back and shoulder from rounding forward.
- Always lift a weight that can be controlled throughout the range of motion.
- Use the same movement with neutral grips for the kettlebell version of this exercise.
- Repeat this movement for the correct number of repetitions and sets required to meet the goal of the free weight session.

Figure 14-15. FW10 Upright Row—straight bar

Figure 14-16. FW10 Upright Row—kettlebell

OVERHEAD PUSH-PRESS

14-19.   The Overhead Push-Press is also performed in the Strength Training Circuit with kettlebells. In this version it is performed with a straight bar, requiring more skill and coordination. Figure 14-17 demonstrates the exercise as it would be conducted by an individual Soldier:

- The starting position for the Overhead Push-Press is the Straddle Stance position with the knees slightly flexed or a Straddle Stance position with staggered legs holding the bar near the top of the chest just below the collar bones. Use a closed overhand grip.
- From the starting position, perform a drop and drive by flexing the knees and hips before forcefully extending them. Simultaneously, extend the elbows and shoulders to raise the bar overhead.
- The neck can slightly extend to allow the bar to pass in front of the face as it moves overhead.
- If the Straddle Stance position with staggered legs is used for the starting position, adjust the feet during the drive phase to the Straddle Stance position. Hold the weight above the head with elbows straight.
- After a brief pause, reverse the movement to return to the down position—flex the elbows, hips, and knees to cushion the impact on the shoulders as the weight descends.
- As the weight and repetitions increase, concentrate on preventing the upper back and shoulders from rounding forward.
- Always lift a weight that can be controlled throughout the range of motion.
- Repeat this movement for the correct number of repetitions and sets required to meet the goal of the free weight session.

Figure 14-17. FW11 Overhead Push-Press

BENT-ARM LATERAL RAISE

14-20.   The Bent-Arm Lateral Raise develops strength in the shoulder and neck muscles. Performing it in the Front Leaning Stance position requires stability of the trunk, lower back, and leg muscles. Figure 14-18 on page 14-16 shows the exercise as it would be conducted by an individual Soldier with dumbbells:

- The starting position for the Bent-Arm Lateral Raise is the Forward Leaning Stance position with the knees slightly flexed holding the dumbbells in front of the thighs using a neutral grip.
- From the starting position, raise the weight to shoulder height while simultaneously bending the elbows to 90 degrees. The rest of the body does not move.
- After a brief pause, reverse the movement to return to the down position—flex the elbows, hips, and knees to cushion the impact on the shoulders as the weight descends.
- As the weight and repetitions increase, concentrate on preventing the upper back and shoulder from rounding forward.

- End in starting position.
- Always lift a weight that can be controlled throughout the range of motion.
- Repeat this movement for the correct number of repetitions and sets required to meet the goal of the free weight session.

Figure 14-18. FW12 Bent-Arm Lateral Raise

SHRUG

14-21. The Shrug is another method of targeting the upper trapezius muscles in the shoulders and neck. The Straight Arm Pull and Upright Row require the same muscles. The Shrug can be performed with a straight bar, dumbbells, or kettlebells. Figure 14-19 breaks down the exercise as a Soldier conducts it using a dumbbells, kettlebells, and straight bar:

- The starting position for the Shrug is the Straddle Stance position with arms fully extended and down in front of the body holding the straight bar, dumbbell, or kettlebell with a closed overhand grip. The knees are slightly flexed.
- From the starting position, raise the weight up by shrugging the shoulders upward.
- After a brief pause, reverse the movement to return to the down position.
- As the weight and repetitions increase, concentrate on preventing the upper back and shoulder from rounding forward.
- Always lift a weight that can be controlled throughout the range of motion.
- Use the same movement with neutral grips for the kettlebell version of this exercise.
- Repeat this movement for the correct number of repetitions and sets required to meet the goal of the free weight session.

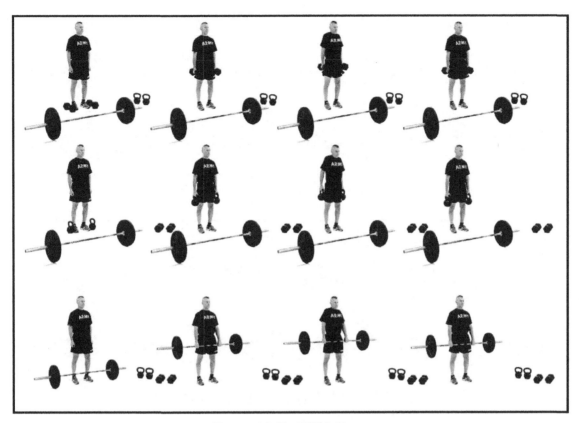

Figure 14-19. FW13 Shrug

PULL OVER

14-22.   The Pull Over develops strength in the triceps muscles which support Free Weight Core exercises like the Bench Press. It is performed using a bench and spotter. Figures 14-20 and 14-21 on page 14-18 show the exercise as it would be conducted by an individual Soldier with single and double dumbbells:

- The spotting position for the Pull Over is the Front Leaning Stance position. The spotter is positioned and maintains hands close to the lifter's hands throughout the movement.
- The starting position for the Pull Over is the Supine position on a bench with feet on the ground, and hips, shoulders, and head firmly resting on the bench.
- A dumbbell is held in each hand, resting on the front of the shoulders. If one dumbbell is used, it rests on the front of the upper chest.
- From the starting position, raise the weight up and past the face until it has cleared the top of the head. Lower the weight down until it is at or below the level of the bench.
- After a brief pause, reverse the movement to return to the starting position.
- Always lift a weight that can be controlled throughout the range of motion.
- Use one weight to improve control if necessary.
- Repeat this movement for the correct number of repetitions and sets required to meet the goal of the free weight session.

Figure 14-20. FW14 Pull Over—single dumbbell

Figure 14-21. FW14 Pull Over—double dumbbells

OVERHEAD TRICEPS EXTENSION

14-23. The Overhead Triceps Extension develops strength in the triceps muscles that support Free Weight Core exercises like the Bench Press. It is performed using a single kettlebell or dumbbell. Figure 14-22 shows the exercise as it would be conducted by an individual Soldier:

- The starting position for the Overhead Triceps Extension is the Straddle Stance position with the arms extended overhead holding a single dumbbell or kettlebell.
- Grip the kettlebell with one hand on either side of the handle with the bell toward the ground.
- Hold the dumbbell by cupping one end of the dumbbell in both hands with the other end toward the floor.
- From the starting position, lower the weight behind the head and between the shoulder blades. Inhale through the movement.
- After a brief pause, reverse the movement to return to the starting position, exhaling through the movement.
- Do not arch the back during the lift and keep the head aligned with the spine.
- Always lift a weight that can be controlled throughout the range of motion.
- Use a lighter weight to improve control if necessary.
- Repeat this movement for the correct number of repetitions and sets required to meet the goal of the free weight session.

Figure 14-22. FW15 Overhead Triceps Extension

BICEPS CURL

14-24. The Biceps Curl develops strength in the biceps muscles which support other free weight and physical training exercises that involve pulling, carrying, and lifting. Other equipment options include a cambered bar, kettlebells, and a climbing bar. To isolate the biceps on the climbing bar during the Pull-Up, switch to a closed, underhand supinated grip. Figure 14-23 on page 14-20 breaks down the exercise as it would be conducted by an individual Soldier with a pair of dumbbells:

- The starting position for the Biceps Curl is the Straddle Stance position with arms straight at the side and a dumbbell in each hand using a neutral grip.
- From the starting position, raise the weights up toward the chest by flexing the elbows. The forearm will supinate or rotate into supination or turn out during the up movement.
- After a brief pause, reverse the movement to lower the weight back to the starting position.
- Always lift a weight that can be controlled throughout the range of motion.
- Repeat this movement for the correct number of repetitions and sets required to meet the goal of the free weight session.

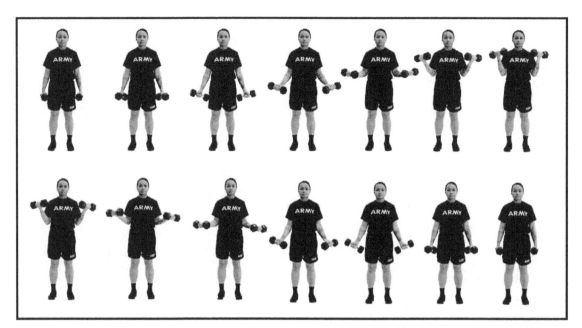

Figure 14-23. FW16 Biceps Curl

WEIGHTED TRUNK FLEXION

14-25.   The Weighted Trunk Flexion develops strength in the abdominal muscles to support trunk movement when the Soldier is wearing full uniform and protective equipment. Figure 14-24 shows the exercise as it would be conducted by an individual Soldier:

- The starting position for the Weighted Trunk Flexion is the Supine position with knees bent to 90 degrees and feet on the ground. Feet are unanchored.
- Hold a dumbbell or plate in each hand, resting on the front of the chest.
- From the starting position, raise the trunk up into a sitting position without shifting the feet and leg position.
- After a brief pause, reverse the movement to return under control to the starting position.
- Always use a weight that can be controlled throughout the range of motion.
- Use a lighter weight to improve control if necessary.
- Repeat this movement for the correct number of repetitions and sets required to meet the goal of the free weight session.

Figure 14-24. FW17 Weighted Trunk Flexion

WEIGHTED TRUNK EXTENSION

14-26.   The Weighted Trunk Extension develops strength in the muscles of the lower back and hips. It is performed using a bench and a partner. Figure 14-25 shows the exercise as a Soldier conducts it:

- To reach the starting position for the Weighted Trunk Extension, lay in the Prone position on a trunk extension bench with the knees slightly flexed and feet anchored or on the end of a flat bench. A partner secures the exerciser's legs at the calves or ankles.
- Hold a weight plate against the chest before lowering the upper body toward the ground by flexing at the hips. This is the starting position.
- From the starting position, raise the upper body to align the trunk with the legs. When viewed from the side, the body and legs will form a straight line from the head to the heels.
- The partner continues to brace the legs throughout the movement.
- After a brief pause, reverse the movement lowering the body back down to the starting position.
- Always lift a weight that can be controlled throughout the range of motion.
- Repeat this movement for the correct number of repetitions and sets required to meet the goal of the free weight session.

Figure 14-25. FW18 Weighted Trunk Extension

This page intentionally left blank.

Chapter 15

Strength Training Machine Drill

STRENGTH TRAINING MACHINES

15-1. Strength Training Machines (known as STMs) are commonly available and frequently used by Soldiers as part of a gym-based reconditioning program or whenever other strength training apparatus is not available. They provide a safe way to isolate muscles or limbs. Paragraphs 15-3 through 15-30 list Strength Training Machines and instructions with generic guidance. They do not have to be used in the order listed. The Strength Training Machine Drill is conducted on strength and mobility days or in accordance with the Soldier's DA Form 3349.

15-2. Videos of Strength Training Machine Drill exercises on the Central Army Registry website at https://atiam.train.army.mil/catalog/search?current=true&filetype=mp4&respect_date=5%2F1%2F2020&search_terms=CIMT demonstrate movements. (Copy and paste this address after accessing the Central Army Registry website if the demonstrations do not populate.) Additional support for H2F test events and exercises are located on the Army Combat Fitness Test website at https://www.army.mil/acft/.

LEG PRESS

15-3. The Leg Press develops strength in the hip and thigh muscles. Figure 15-1 on page 15-2 breaks down the exercise as it would be conducted by an individual Soldier:
- The starting position for the Leg Press is the Sitting position with the knees bent at 90 degrees and feet flat on the foot platform.
- Place the hips, low back, shoulders, and head firmly against the seat back with the eyes looking straight ahead.
- Maintain a natural arch in the lower back.
- Select the appropriate weight and ensure the pin is secure in the weight stack.
- Keep hands relaxed and placed on the handgrips.
- On count 1, straighten the legs slowly until they are fully extended but not locked.
- On count 2, return to the starting position in a slow, controlled motion.
- Repeat this movement for the correct number of repetitions and sets required to meet the goal of the strength machine session.

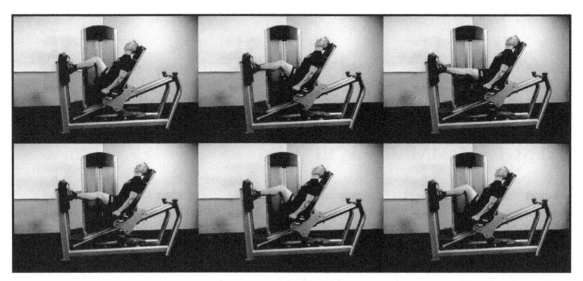

Figure 15-1. STM Leg Press

MODIFIED LEG PRESS

15-4. The modified Leg Press is performed the same as the leg press. However, Soldiers use a smaller range of motion. As a Soldier's condition improves, the range of motion and resistance may gradually increase until the exercise is performed to standard. However, do not increase both of these factors at the same time.

SINGLE-LEG PRESS

15-5. The Single-Leg Press is performed much like the leg press, only one leg at a time (see figure 15-2). The range of motion and resistance is decreased for the injured leg. As a Soldier's condition improves, the range of motion and resistance may gradually increase until the exercise is performed to standard. However, do not increase both of these factors at the same time. The Single-Leg Press is used to maintain a heavy resistance on the good leg, to reduce the resistance on the injured leg, or both.

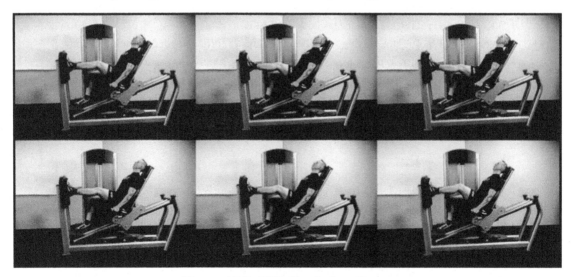

Figure 15-2. STM Single-Leg Press

LEG CURL

15-6. The Leg Curl is the second exercise in the Strength Training Machine drill. This exercise develops strength in the back of the upper leg muscles. Figure 15-3 shows the exercise as a Soldier conducts it:

- The starting position for the Leg Curl is the Prone position, knees aligned with the center axis of the machine.
- Adjust the lower leg pad to contact the lower legs just above and behind the ankle, allowing the lower legs to be fully extended.
- Relax the lower legs and feet. Position the thigh pad just above and in front of the knees.
- Place the hips, stomach, and chest firmly against the bench with the eyes looking straight down.
- Select the appropriate weight and ensure the pin is secure in the weight stack.
- Relax hands and place them on the handgrips.
- On count 1, slowly pull the lower legs to the rear toward the buttocks.
- On count 2, return to the starting position by slowly lowering the lower legs.
- Repeat this movement for the correct number of repetitions and sets required to meet the goal of the strength machine session.

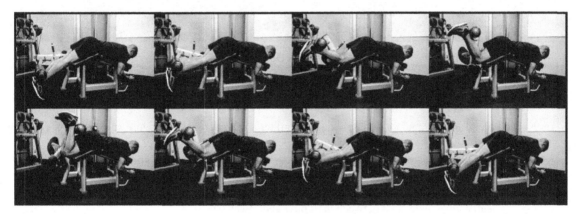

Figure 15-3. STM Leg Curl

MODIFIED LEG CURL

15-7. The modified Leg Curl is performed in the Prone position through a limited range of motion. Soldiers with low back or hip injuries may prefer to use the seated leg curl if it is available. A Soldier conducts the exercise doing the following:

- The starting position for the Leg Curl is the Prone position, knees aligned with the center axis of the machine.
- Keep the chest flat on the bench. The legs may be extended or partially flexed. Grab the handles of the machine.
- From the starting position, curl the legs up as far as possible without lifting your upper legs from the pad.
- Pause for a second, then return the legs slowly to the starting position.
- Repeat this movement for the correct number of repetitions and sets required to meet the goal of the strength machine session.

SINGLE-LEG CURL

15-8. The Single-Leg Curl is performed in the Prone position using only one leg at a time (see figure 15-4). As the Soldier's condition improves, the range of motion and resistance may gradually increase until the exercise is performed to standard. However, do not increase both of these factors at the same time. The Single-Leg Curl is used to maintain a heavy resistance on the good leg, reduce the resistance on the injured leg, or decrease the range of motion on the injured leg.

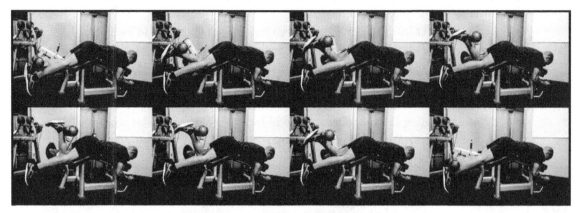

Figure 15-4. STM Single-Leg Curl

LATERAL RAISE

15-9. The Lateral Raise develops strength in the shoulder and neck muscles. Figure 15-5 shows the exercise as it would be conducted by an individual Soldier:

- The starting position for the Lateral Raise is the Sitting position with the knees bent at 90 degrees and feet flat on the floor.
- From the starting position, stay seated with the feet firmly on the ground. Adjust the seat so a 90-degree angle is formed between the upper and lower arms.
- Place the hips, lower back, shoulders, and head firmly against the seat back with the eyes looking straight ahead.
- Maintain a natural arch in the lower back.
- Select the appropriate weight and ensure the pin is secure in the weight stack.
- On count 1, raise both arms upward until they are parallel to the ground.
- On count 2, return to the starting position.
- Repeat this movement for the correct number of repetitions and sets required to meet the goal of the strength machine session.

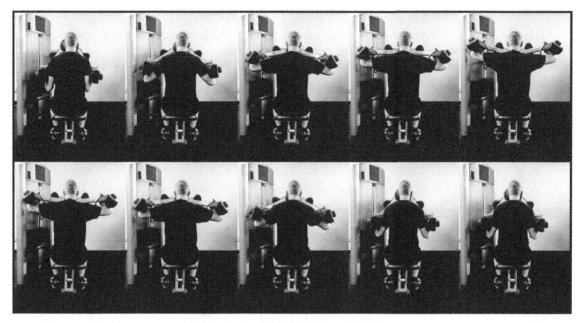

Figure 15-5. STM Lateral Raise

SINGLE-ARM LATERAL RAISE

15-10.   The Single-Arm Lateral Raise is performed much like the Lateral Raise but using only one arm at a time (see figure 15-6). The range of motion and resistance is decreased for the injured side. As the Soldier's condition improves, the range of motion and resistance may gradually increase until the exercise is performed to standard. However, do not increase both of these factors at the same time. The Single-Arm Lateral Raise is used to maintain a heavy resistance on the good side, reduce the resistance on the injured side, or both.

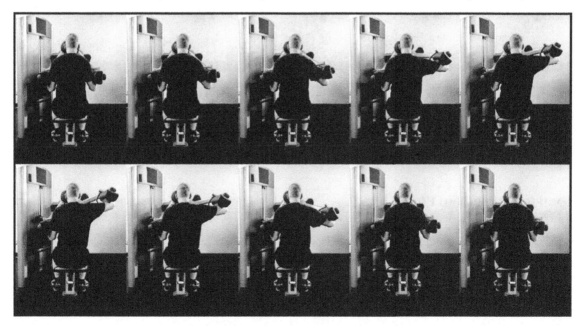

Figure 15-6. STM Single-Arm Lateral Raise

OVERHEAD PRESS

15-11. The Overhead Press develops strength in the arm and shoulder muscles. Figure 15-7 breaks down the exercise as it would be conducted by an individual Soldier:

- The starting position for the Overhead Press is the Sitting position with the knees bent at 90 degrees and feet flat on the floor.
- From the starting position, stay seated with the feet firmly on the ground.
- Adjust the seat to achieve a 90-degree angle between the Soldier's upper and lower arms with the shoulders directly below the handgrips.
- Place the hips, low back, and shoulders firmly against the seat back.
- Look straight ahead.
- On count 1, push upward until both arms are fully extended but not locked.
- On count 2, return to the starting position.
- Repeat this movement for the correct number of repetitions and sets required to meet the goal of the strength machine session.

Figure 15-7. STM Overhead Press

MODIFIED OVERHEAD PRESS

15-12. The modified Overhead Press is performed the same as the Overhead Press but with a smaller range of motion. Soldiers do not flex the elbows below 90 degrees as they lower resistance is lowered, nor will they fully straighten when the resistance is raised. As the Soldier's condition improves, the range of motion and resistance may gradually increase until the exercise is performed to standard. However, these two factors should not be increased at the same time.

SINGLE-ARM OVERHEAD PRESS

15-13. The Single-Arm Overhead Press is performed much like the Overhead Press, using one arm at a time (see figure 15-8). The range of motion and resistance is decreased for the injured side. As the Soldier's condition improves, the range of motion may gradually increase until the exercise is performed to standard. The resistance should not be increased until the Soldier can move through the full range of motion and perform the exercise to standard. The Single-Arm Overhead Press is used to maintain a heavy resistance on the good side, reduce the resistance on the injured side, or both.

Figure 15-8. STM Single-Arm Overhead Press

LAT PULL-DOWN

15-14. The Lat Pull-Down is the fifth exercise in the strength training machine drill. This exercise develops strength in the arm and back muscles. Figure 15-9 on page 15-8 shows the exercise as a Soldier conducts it:

- The starting position for the Lat Pull-Down is the Sitting position with the knees bent at 90 degrees and feet flat on the floor.
- From the starting position, select the appropriate weight and ensure the pin is secure in the weight stack.
- Sit erect and adjust the roller pad so it sits firmly against the upper thigh and hip.
- Grasp the bar with a closed, pronated grip and assume a Sitting position with the hips against the roller pad and the feet flat on the ground.
- Check the upper body is perpendicular to the floor.
- On count 1, keeping the arms straight and elbows rotated out to the side and slightly flexed, simultaneously bend the elbows and pull the bar toward the shoulders until the upper arms are parallel to the ground.
- On count 2, return to the starting position by slowly extending the elbows.
- Repeat this movement for the correct number of repetitions and sets required to meet the goal of the strength machine session.

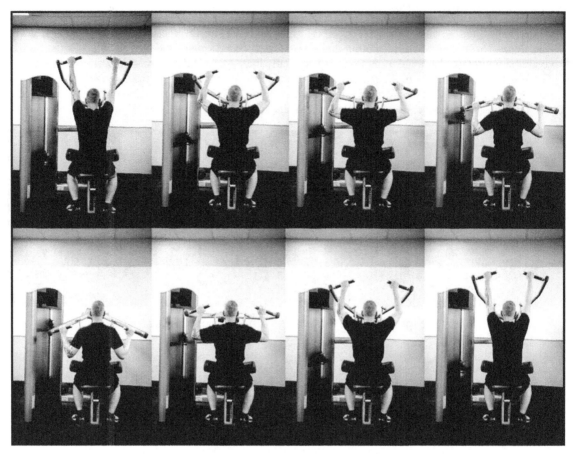

Figure 15-9. STM Lat Pull-Down

STRAIGHT-ARM LAT PULL-DOWN

15-15.   The Straight-Arm Lat Pull-Down is performed the same as the Lat Pull-Down. However, it uses a much smaller range of motion. The elbows remain fully extended and the arms straight. As with the Straight-Arm Pull exercise in Climbing Drill 1 (see paragraph 6-3), the movement has the effect of raising the head between the arms. The chest will move up toward the bar and the shoulder blades will move together.

SINGLE-ARM LAT PULL-DOWN

15-16.   The Single-Arm Lat Pull-Down is performed much like the Lat Pull-Down, using only one arm at a time (see figure 15-10). The range of motion and resistance is decreased for the injured side. As the Soldier's condition improves, the range of motion and resistance may gradually increase until the exercise is performed to standard. However, do not increase both of these factors at the same time. The Single-Arm Lat Pull-Down is used to maintain a heavy resistance on the good side, reduce the resistance on the injured side, or both.

Figure 15-10. STM Single-Arm Lat Pull-Down

SEATED ROW

15-17. The Seated Row develops strength in the arm and back muscles. Figure 15-11 on page 15-10 shows the exercise as it would be conducted by an individual Soldier:

- The starting position for the Seated Row is the Sitting position with the knees bent at 90 degrees and feet flat on the floor.
- From the starting position, stay seated with the feet firmly planted on the floor or foot supports (if using).
- Lean forward and grasp the handgrips with the hands in a neutral, closed grip.
- Sit erect so the upper body is perpendicular to the floor.
- Select the appropriate weight and ensure the pin is secure in the weight stack.
- On count 1, simultaneously bend the elbows and pull the handgrips to the chest or upper abdomen while keeping the trunk rigid and the back flat.

- On count 2, return to the starting position by slowly extending the elbows.
- Repeat this movement for the correct number of repetitions and sets required to meet the goal of the strength machine session.

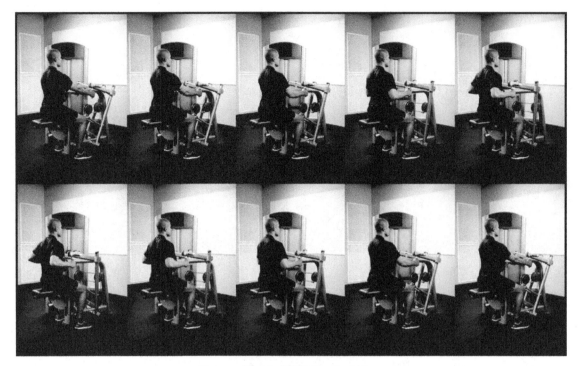

Figure 15-11. STM Seated Row

STRAIGHT-ARM SEATED ROW

15-18.   The Straight-Arm Seated Row is performed the same as the Seated Row. However, it uses a much smaller range of motion. The elbows remain fully extended and the arms straight as the resistance is lowered or raised.

SINGLE-ARM SEATED ROW

15-19.   The Single-Arm Seated Row is performed much like the Seated Row, using only one arm at a time (see figure 15-12). The range of motion and resistance is decreased for the injured side. As the Soldier's condition improves, the range of motion and resistance may gradually increase until the exercise is performed to standard. However, do not increase both of these factors at the same time. The Single-Arm Seated Row is used to maintain a heavy resistance on the good side, reduce the resistance on the injured side, or both.

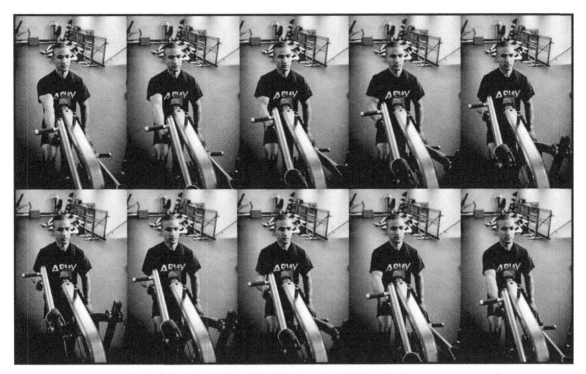

Figure 15-12. STM Single-Arm Seated Row

TRUNK EXTENSION

15-20.   The Trunk Extension is the seventh exercise in the Strength Training Machine drill. This exercise develops strength in the low back muscles and supports the Deadlift exercise. Figure 15-13 on page 15-12 shows the exercise as a Soldier conducts it:

- The starting position for the Trunk Extension is the Sitting position with the knees slightly bent and feet flat on the foot platform.
- From the starting position, stay seated on the machine, leaning slightly forward, with the back firmly against the padded lever arm.
- Select the appropriate weight and ensure the pin is secure in the weight stack.
- Grip the support bars using a neutral, closed grip.
- Keep the head in a neutral position with the eyes looking straight ahead.
- On count 1, raise the upper body and continue extending the trunk, moving to the Supine position.
- On count 2, return to the starting position.
- Repeat this movement for the correct number of repetitions and sets required to meet the goal of the strength machine session.

Figure 15-13. STM Trunk Extension

MODIFIED TRUNK EXTENSION

15-21.   The modified Trunk Extension should be used when a DA Form 3349 may limit the range of motion at which a Soldier can safely perform Trunk Extension exercises. The weight load should be low and the range of motion of the movements should be within the comfort zone of the Soldier. Gradually increase the weight load and range of motion as tolerated until the exercise can be performed to standard.

TRICEPS EXTENSION

15-22.   The Triceps Extension develops strength in the triceps muscles and supports other pushing tasks found in training and combat. Figure 15-14 breaks down the exercise as a Soldier conducts it:

- Select the weight and ensure the pin is secure in the weight stack.
- Conduct this exercise from the Sitting position. Start with the feet placed firmly on the ground. Place the hips and low back firmly against the seat back with the eyes looking straight ahead.
- Maintain an erect position, eyes looking straight ahead, grasping the bar with a closed, pronated grip.
- On count 1, push downward until both arms are fully extended but not locked.
- On count 2, return to the starting position.
- Repeat this movement for the correct number of repetitions and sets required to meet the goal of the strength machine session.

Figure 15-14. STM Triceps Extension

MODIFIED TRICEPS EXTENSION

15-23.   The modified Triceps Extension is performed the same as the triceps extension, but it uses a smaller range of motion. The elbows will not fully flex as the resistance is lowered, nor will they fully straighten when the resistance is raised.

15-24.   As the Soldier's condition improves, the range of motion and resistance may gradually increase until the exercise is performed to standard. However, do not increase both of these factors at the same time.

SINGLE-ARM TRICEPS EXTENSION

15-25.   The Single-Arm Triceps Extension is performed much like the triceps extension, using only one arm at a time (see figure 15-15). The range of motion and resistance is decreased for the injured side. As the Soldier's condition improves, the range of motion and resistance may gradually increase until the exercise is performed to standard. However, do not increase both of these factors at the same time. The single arm triceps extension is used to maintain a heavy resistance on the good side, reduce the resistance on the injured side, or both.

Figure 15-15. STM Single-Arm Triceps Extension

CHEST PRESS

15-26.   The Chest Press develops strength in the arms, shoulders, and chest muscles. Figure 15-16 on page 15-14 breaks down the exercise as a Soldier conducts it:
- The starting position for the Chest Press is the Sitting position with the knees bent at 90 degrees and feet flat on the floor.
- From the starting position, stay seated with the feet firmly on the ground. Adjust the seat so a 90-degree angle is formed between the upper and lower arms with the shoulders directly below the handgrips.
- Place the hips, low back, shoulders, and head firmly against the seat back with the eyes looking straight ahead.
- Maintain a natural arch in the lower back.
- Select the appropriate weight and ensure the pin is secure in the weight stack.
- On count 1, push upward until the arms are fully extended but not locked.
- On count 2, return to the starting position.
- Repeat this movement for the correct number of repetitions and sets required to meet the goal of the strength machine session.

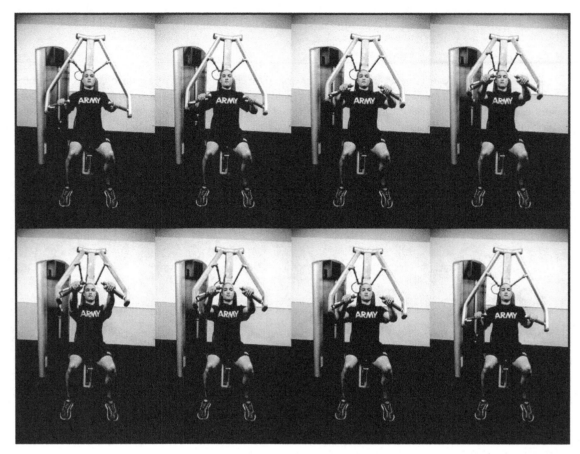

Figure 15-16. STM Chest Press

MODIFIED CHEST PRESS

15-27.   The modified Chest Press is performed the same as the chest press, but it uses a much smaller range of motion. The elbows will not flex below 90 degrees as the resistance is lowered, nor will they fully straighten when the resistance is raised. As the Soldier's condition improves, the range of motion and resistance may gradually increase until the exercise is performed to standard. However, do not increase both of these factors at the same time.

SINGLE-ARM CHEST PRESS

15-28.   The Single-Arm Chest Press is performed in the same way as the Chest Press, using only one arm at a time (see figure 15-17). The range of motion and resistance is decreased for the injured side. The Single-Arm Chest Press is used to maintain a heavy resistance on the good side, reduce the resistance on the injured side, or both.

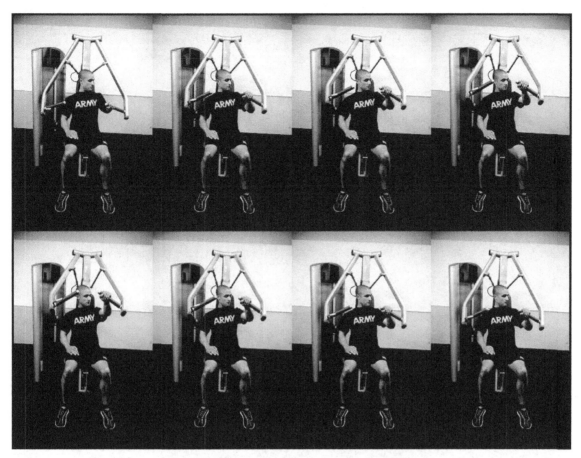

Figure 15-17. STM Single-Arm Chest Press

TRUNK FLEXION

15-29.   The Trunk Flexion is the tenth exercise in the strength training machine drill. This exercise develops strength in the abdominal muscles. Figure 15-18 on page 15-16 shows the exercise as a Soldier conducts it:

- The starting position for the Trunk Flexion is the Sitting position with the knees bent at 90 degrees and feet flat on the floor.
- From the starting position, stay seated with the feet firmly on the ground.
- Select the appropriate weight and ensure the pin is secure in the weight stack.
- Keep the elbows shoulder-width apart and bent at 90 degrees, with hands in a closed grip.
- Place the hips and low back firmly against the seat back with the eyes looking straight ahead.
- On count 1, bend forward, flexing the trunk and bringing the chest to the thighs.
- On count 2, return to the starting position.

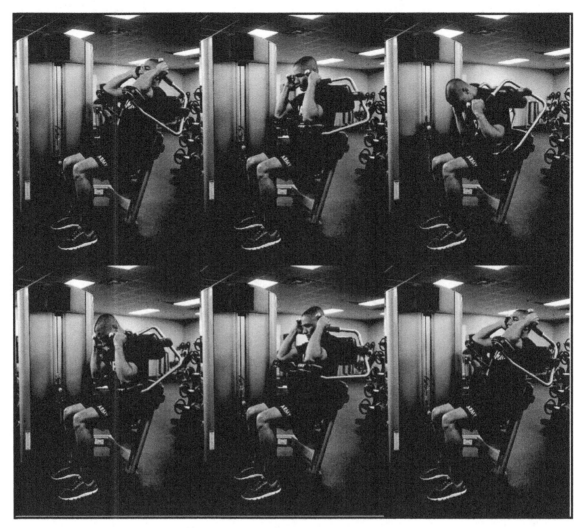

Figure 15-18. STM Trunk Flexion

MODIFIED TRUNK FLEXION

15-30. The modified Trunk Flexion should be used when a DA Form 3349 may limit the range of motion at which a Soldier can safely perform Trunk Flexion exercises. The weight load should be low and the range of motion of the movements should be within the comfort zone of the Soldier. Gradually increase the weight load and range of motion as tolerated until the exercise can be performed to standard.

Chapter 16

Recovery Drills

THE RECOVERY DRILL

16-1. The Recovery Drill (known as RD) includes a wide variety of range of movements that require structural strength, stability, flexibility, and mobility. Positions include Sitting, Standing, Prone, and Supine positions supported by one or both upper and lower extremities. Movements into and out of these positions can be modified to accommodate Soldiers who are reconditioning from injury, who are deconditioned, or who are new to the Army.

16-2. Videos of Recovery Drill exercises located on the Central Army Registry website at https://atiam.train.army.mil/catalog/search?current=true&filetype=mp4&respect_date=5%2F1%2F2020&search_terms=CIMT demonstrate movements. (Copy and paste this address after accessing the Central Army Registry website if the demonstrations do not populate.) Additional support for H2F test events and exercises are located on the Army Combat Fitness Test website at https://www.army.mil/acft/.

1. OVERHEAD ARM PULL

16-3. The Overhead Arm Pull is the first exercise in the Recovery Drill. This exercise develops the flexibility of joints in the arms, shoulders, and trunk. Figure 16-1 illustrates the movement as Soldiers conduct it in a formation:

- The starting position for the Overhead Arm Pull is the Straddle Stance position with hands on hips. When commanded, "READY, *STRETCH*," raise the left arm overhead. Grasp above the left elbow with the right hand and pull to the right, leaning the body to the right. A stretch sensation should be felt in the left triceps muscle and flank. Hold this position for 20–30 seconds.
- On the command, "STARTING POSITION, *MOVE*," return to the starting position.
- On the command, "CHANGE POSITION, READY, *STRETCH*," repeat the movement on the right side.
- On the command, "STARTING POSITION, *MOVE*," return to the starting position.

Figure 16-1. RD1 Overhead Arm Pull

2. REAR LUNGE

16-4. The Rear Lunge is the second exercise in the Recovery Drill. Figure 16-2 demonstrates the movement as Soldiers conduct it in a formation:

- The starting position for the Rear Lunge is the Straddle Stance position with hands on hips.
- On the command, "READY, *STRETCH*," take an exaggerated step backward with the left leg, touching down with the ball of the foot directly behind the starting position. This creates a stretch sensation in the front of the left thigh and hip area. Back remains straight and gaze remains forward. Hold the position for 20–30 seconds.
- On the command, "STARTING POSITION, *MOVE*," return to the starting position.
- On the command, "READY, *STRETCH*," take an exaggerated step backward with the right leg, touching down with the ball of the foot directly behind the starting position. This creates a stretch sensation in the front of the right thigh and hip area. The back remains straight and gaze remains forward. Hold the position for 20–30 seconds.
- On the command, "STARTING POSITION, *MOVE*," return to the starting position.

Figure 16-2. RD2 Rear Lunge

3. EXTEND AND FLEX

16-5. The Extend and Flex is the third exercise in the Recovery Drill. Figure 16-3 breaks down the movement as Soldiers conduct it in a formation:

- The starting position for the Extend and Flex is the Front Leaning Rest position.
- On the command, "READY, *STRETCH*," lower the body toward the ground, sagging in the middle while keeping the arms straight. Keep gaze straight ahead—do not look up. This creates a stretch sensation in the hip and abdominal muscles. The legs and low back should be relaxed with toes on the ground and pointing to the rear. Hold the position for 20–30 seconds.
- On the command, "STARTING POSITION, *MOVE*," return to the starting position.
- On the command, "CHANGE POSITION, READY, *STRETCH*," put bodyweight back on the balls of the feet to support raising the hips up and off the ground. Straighten the legs and try to touch the ground with the heels. Move the head between the arms and look toward the feet. The back remains straight. Hold the position for 20–30 seconds.
- On the command, "STARTING POSITION, *MOVE*," return to the starting position.

Figure 16-3. RD3 Extend and Flex

4. THIGH STRETCH

16-6. The Thigh Stretch is the fourth exercise in the Recovery Drill. It develops flexibility in the hip and knee joints. Figure 16-4 shows the movement as Soldiers conduct it in a formation:

- The starting position for the Thigh Stretch is the Sitting position with the arms at the sides and palms on the floor.
- On the command, "READY, *STRETCH*," roll on the right side and place the right elbow and forearm on the ground directly below the shoulder. The right hand makes a fist with the thumb side up. Grasp the left ankle and pull toward the left buttock. Push the left thigh further to the rear with the heel of the right foot. Hold this position for 20–30 seconds.
- On the command, "CHANGE POSITION, READY, *STRETCH*," move back through the starting position before changing sides to stretch the right leg. Hold for 20–30 seconds.
- On the command, "STARTING POSITION, *MOVE*," return to the starting position.

Figure 16-4. RD4 Thigh Stretch

5. SINGLE-LEG OVER

16-7. The Single-Leg Over is the fifth exercise in Recovery Drill. This exercise develops flexibility of the hip and low back. Figure 16-5 breaks down the movement as Soldiers conduct it in a formation for 30–60 seconds:

- The starting position for the Single-Leg Over is the Supine position with arms straight out to the side on ground with palms down with fingers and thumbs extended and joined. Feet are together with heels on the ground. The head is on the ground.
- On the command, "READY, *STRETCH*," bend the left knee to 90 degrees over the right leg and grasp the outside of the left knee with the right hand pulling toward the right. Keep the left shoulder and arm on the ground. Hold this position for 20–30 seconds.
- On the command, "STARTING POSITION, *MOVE*," assume the starting position.
- On the command, "CHANGE POSITION, READY, *STRETCH*," bend the right knee to 90 degrees over the left leg and grasp the outside of the right knee with the left hand pulling toward the left. Keep the right shoulder and arm on the ground. Hold this position for 20–30 seconds.
- On the command, "STARTING POSITION, *MOVE*," return to the starting position.

Figure 16-5. RD5 Single-Leg Over

6. GROIN STRETCH

16-8. The Groin Stretch is the sixth exercise in the Recovery Drill. This exercise increases flexibility in the hip joint. Figure 16-6 shows the movement as Soldiers conduct it in a formation:

- The starting position for the Groin Stretch is the Straddle Stance position with hands on hips.
- On the command, "READY, *STRETCH*," take an exaggerated step with the right leg to the right side bending the right knee into a lateral lunge. Trunk and head continue to face forward. Hold this position or continue into a deeper lunge to stretch the inside of the left thigh for 20–30 seconds.
- On the command, "STARTING POSITION, *MOVE*," assume the starting position.
- On the command, "CHANGE POSITION, READY, *STRETCH*," take an exaggerated step to the left with the left leg bending the left knee into a lateral lunge. Trunk and head continue to face

forward. Hold the position or continue into a deeper lunge to stretch the inside of the right thigh for 20–30 seconds.

- On count 4, return to the starting position.

Figure 16-6. RD6 Groin Stretch

7. CALF STRETCH

16-9. The Calf Stretch is the seventh exercise in Recovery Drill. This stretch increases flexibility of the ankle. Figure 16-7 illustrates the movement as Soldiers conduct it in a formation:

- The starting position for the Calf Stretch is the Straddle Stance position with hands on hips.
- On the command, "READY, *STRETCH*," take a step backward with the left leg, placing the foot flat on the ground 1–2 feet behind its starting position. Keeping the left heel on the ground, bend both knees until a stretch is felt in the left Achilles tendon.
- On the command, "STARTING POSITION, *MOVE*," return to the starting position.
- On the command, "READY, *STRETCH*," repeat the stretch with the right leg. Increase the stretch sensation in the right calf muscle by stepping further back with the right foot and locking the right knee. Keep the right foot pointing forward throughout the stretch. Hold either stretch position for 20–30 seconds.
- On the command, "STARTING POSITION, *MOVE*," return to the starting position.

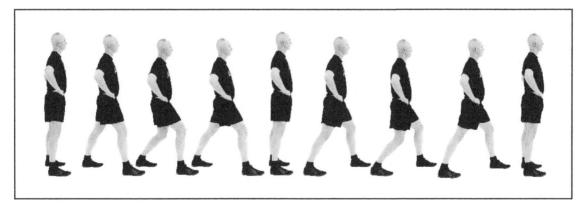

Figure 16-7. RD7 Calf Stretch

8. HAMSTRING STRETCH

16-10.   The Hamstring Stretch is the final exercise in Recovery Drill. This stretch increases flexibility of the knees and hips. Figure 16-8 breaks down the movement as Soldiers conduct it in a formation:

- The starting position for the Hamstring Stretch is the Sitting position with arms at the sides and palms on the floor.
- On the command, "READY, *STRETCH*," reach forward with both hands toward the feet, grasping the feet, ankle or lower legs. Keep the knees straight without locking them. Hold this stretch position for 20–30 seconds.
- On the command, "STARTING POSITION, *MOVE*," return to the starting position.
- On the command, "READY, *STRETCH*," repeat the first stretch position reaching slightly further.
- On the command, "STARTING POSITION, *MOVE*," return to the starting position.

Figure 16-8. RD8 Hamstring Stretch

THE RECOVERY DRILL (MODIFIED)

16-11.   The Recovery Drill (Modified) (known as RD MOD) includes the same exercises as those described in the Recovery Drill but with restricted range of motion to accommodate for injury. Positions include modified Sitting, Standing, Prone, and Supine positions supported by one or both upper and lower extremities. Recovery Drill (Modified) exercises are ideal for Soldiers who are reconditioning from injury, who are deconditioned, or who are new to the Army.

1. OVERHEAD ARM PULL (MODIFIED)

16-12.   The Overhead Arm Pull can be modified by stretching the arms across the upper body instead of overhead. If possible, perform the standard stretch on the uninjured arm. Figure 16-9 illustrates the movement as Soldiers conduct it in a formation:

- The starting position for the modified Overhead Arm Pull is the Straddle Stance position with hands on hips.
- When commanded, "READY, *STRETCH*," raise the left arm across the front of the chest. Grasp above the left elbow with the right hand and pull to the right, leaning the body to the right. A stretch sensation should be felt in the left triceps muscle and flank. Hold this position for 20–30 seconds.
- On the command, "STARTING POSITION, *MOVE*" return to the starting position.
- On the command, "CHANGE POSITION, READY, *STRETCH*," repeat the movement on the right side.
- On the command, "STARTING POSITION, *MOVE*," return to the starting position, and then to the Position of Attention.

Figure 16-9. RD MOD1 Overhead Arm Pull (modified)

2. REAR LUNGE (MODIFIED)

16-13.   The Rear Lunge can be modified by reducing the range of motion for the lunge or by stepping forward into the lunge. If possible, perform the standard stretch on the uninjured leg. Figure 16-10 on page 16-8 breaks down the movement as Soldiers conduct it in a formation:

- The starting position for the modified Rear Lunge is the Straddle Stance position with hands on hips.
- On the command, "READY, *STRETCH*," take a step backward with the left leg, touching down with the ball of the foot directly behind the starting position. Keep the trunk erect and move the pelvis forward. This creates a stretch sensation in the front of the left thigh and hip area. The back remains straight and gaze remains forward. Hold the position for 20–30 seconds.
- On the command, "STARTING POSITION, *MOVE*," return to the starting position.
- On the command, "READY, *STRETCH*," repeat the first movement on the right side.
- On the command, "STARTING POSITION, *MOVE*," return to the starting position, and then to the Position of Attention.

Figure 16-10. RD MOD2 Rear Lunge (modified)

3. EXTEND AND FLEX (MODIFIED)

16-14.   The Extend and Flex can be modified by reducing weight placed on the arms, by limiting the range of motion, or by remaining standing and arching the spine forward and backward. Figure 16-11 shows the modification from a starting position of a Six-Point Stance position Soldiers conduct it in a formation:

- The starting position for the modified Extend and Flex is the Front Leaning Rest position.
- On the command, "READY, *STRETCH*," lower the body toward the ground, sagging in the middle and bending the elbows so that the forearms rest on the ground. Keep the gaze straight ahead—do not look up. Keep legs and low back relaxed with toes on the ground and pointing to the rear. Hold the position for 20–30 seconds.
- On the command, "STARTING POSITION, *MOVE*," return to the starting position.
- On the command, "CHANGE POSITION, READY, *STRETCH*," keep the hands in place on the ground and slide the trunk and pelvis rearward. Let the knees bend until the buttocks rest on the back of the legs. Keep the head near to the ground to flex the spine and upper back while the arms remain overhead on the ground. Hold the position for 20–30 seconds.
- On the command, "STARTING POSITION, *MOVE*," return to the starting position, and then to the Position of Attention.

16-15.   The standing position for the modified Extend and Flex avoids weight bearing on the arms, but should not be used in cases of injury to the low back. Figure 16-12 breaks down the movement from a starting Position of Attention as Soldiers conduct it in a formation:

- Place hands on the low back prior to bending backward, and on the front of the thighs prior to bending forward.
- Move in and out of this position for 20–30 seconds or hold for 10–15 seconds and repeat one time.

Figure 16-11. RD MOD3 Extend and Flex (modified)

Figure 16-12. RD MOD3 Extend and Flex (modified)—standing

4. THIGH STRETCH (MODIFIED)

16-16.   The Thigh Stretch can be modified by reducing the knee range of motion. Figure 16-13 breaks down the movement as Soldiers conduct it in a formation:

- The starting position for the modified Thigh Stretch is the Sitting position with the arms at the sides and palms on the floor.
- On the command, "READY, *STRETCH*," roll on the right side and place the right elbow and forearm on the ground directly below the shoulder. Fist the right hand with the thumb up. Grasp the left ankle and pull toward the left buttock. Ensure the right leg remains straight. Hold this position for 20–30 seconds.
- On the command, "CHANGE POSITION, READY, *STRETCH*," move back through the starting position before changing sides to stretch the right leg. Hold for 20–30 seconds.
- On the command, "STARTING POSITION, *MOVE*," return to the starting position, and then to the Position of Attention.

Figure 16-13. RD MOD4 Thigh Stretch (modified)

5. SINGLE-LEG OVER (MODIFIED)

16-17.   The Single-Leg Over can be modified by decreasing the range of motion, by stretching only one leg, or by modifying the position of the stretch. Figure 16-14 illustrates the modified movement as Soldiers conduct it in a formation for 30–60 seconds:

- The starting position for the modified Single-Leg Over is the Supine position with the head on the ground, arms at a 45-degree angle, hips and knees bent with feet on the ground. The knees are bent at 90 degrees and the feet are together.
- On the command, "READY, *STRETCH*," rotate the hips to the right and lower the knees toward the ground. Keep the left shoulder and arm on the ground. Hold this position for 20–30 seconds.
- On the command, "STARTING POSITION, *MOVE*," assume the starting position.
- On the command, "CHANGE POSITION, READY, *STRETCH*," rotate the hips to the left and lower the knees toward the ground. Keep the right shoulder and arm on the ground. Hold this position for 20–30 seconds.
- On the command, "STARTING POSITION, *MOVE*," return to the starting position and then to the Position of Attention.

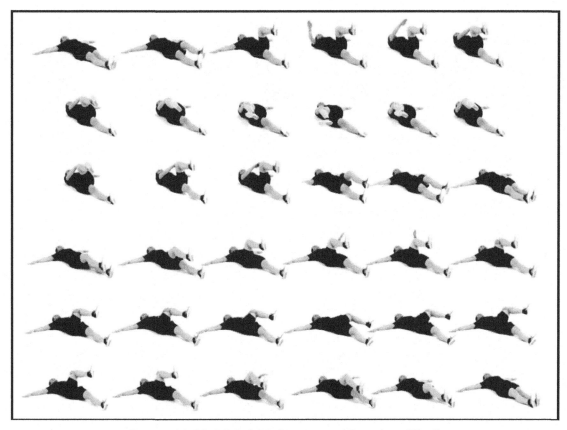

Figure 16-14. RD MOD5 Single-Leg Over (modified)

6. GROIN STRETCH (MODIFIED)

16-18.   The Groin Stretch can be modified by using smaller movements to help increase flexibility in the hip joint. Figure 16-15 on page 16-12 illustrates the movement as Soldiers conduct it in a formation:

- The starting position for the modified Groin Stretch is the Straddle Stance position with hands on hips.
- On the command, "READY, *STRETCH*," take a small step with the left leg to the left side bending the left knee into a lateral lunge. Trunk and head continue to face forward. Hold this position or continue into a deeper lunge to stretch the inside of the right thigh for 20–30 seconds.
- On the command, "STARTING POSITION, *MOVE*," assume the starting position.
- On the command, "CHANGE POSITION, READY, *STRETCH*," take a small step to the right with the right leg bending the right knee into a lateral lunge. Trunk and head continue to face forward. Hold this position or continue into a deeper lunge to stretch the inside of the left thigh for 20–30 seconds.
- On the command, "STARTING POSITION, *MOVE*," return to the starting position and then to the Position of Attention.

Figure 16-15. RD MOD6 Groin Stretch (modified)

7. CALF STRETCH (MODIFIED)

16-19.   The modified Calf Stretch is the seventh exercise in the Recovery Drill (Modified). This stretch increases flexibility of the ankle. Figure 16-16 shows the movement as Soldiers conduct it in a formation:

- The starting position for the modified Calf Stretch is the Straddle Stance position with hands on hips.
- On the command, "READY, *STRETCH*," take a step backward with the left leg, placing the foot flat on the ground 1–2 feet behind its starting position. Keeping the left heel on the ground, bend both knees until a stretch is felt in the left Achilles tendon.
- On the command, "STARTING POSITION, *MOVE*," return to the starting position.
- On the command, "READY, *STRETCH*," repeat the stretch with the right leg. Keep the right foot pointing forward throughout the stretch. Hold either stretch position for 20–30 seconds.
- On the command, "STARTING POSITION, *MOVE*," return to the starting position, and then to the Position of Attention.

Figure 16-16. RD MOD7 Calf Stretch (modified)

8. HAMSTRING STRETCH (MODIFIED)

16-20.   The modified Hamstring Stretch is the final exercise in Recovery Drill (Modified). This stretch increases flexibility of the knee and hip. Figure 16-17 shows one modified movement as Soldiers conduct it in a formation:

- The starting position for the modified Hamstring Stretch is the Sitting position, arms at the sides and palms on the floor.
- On the command, "READY, *STRETCH*," reach forward with both hands until a stretch is felt in the back of the thigh. Keep the knees straight without locking them. Hold this stretch position for 20–30 seconds.
- On the command, "STARTING POSITION, *MOVE*," return to the starting position.
- On the command, "READY, *STRETCH*," repeat the first stretch position, reaching slightly further.
- On the command, "STARTING POSITION, *MOVE*," return to the starting position.

16-21.   Figure 16-18 shows the single-leg Hamstring Stretch. The Soldier bends one knee while keeping the other straight and reaches toward the foot until a stretch is felt in the back of the thigh. Hold this stretch position on each side for 20–30 seconds.

Figure 16-17. RD MOD8 Hamstring (modified)

Figure 16-18. RD MOD8 Hamstring (modified)—single leg

This page intentionally left blank.

Chapter 17

Preventive Maintenance Checks and Services Drills

PREVENTIVE MAINTENANCE CHECKS AND SERVICES

17-1. Preventive Maintenance Checks and Services (PMCS) Drill is a series of exercises that a Soldier can conduct before physical readiness training or as an enhancement to the stretches performed in the Recovery Drill. The purpose of the PMCS Drill is to check for stiffness or pain around a joint and provide a safe and simple way for a Soldier to reduce pain and restore proper movement. If these exercises do not alleviate the issue, Soldiers then seek help from performance readiness experts in their unit.

17-2. Demonstration videos of PMCS exercises are located on the Central Army Registry website at https://atiam.train.army.mil/catalog/search?current=true&filetype=mp4&respect_date=5%2F1%2F2020&search_terms=CIMT. (Copy and paste this address after accessing the Central Army Registry website if the demonstrations do not populate.) Additional support for H2F test events and exercises are located on the Army Combat Fitness Test website at https://www.army.mil/acft/.

1. SPINE

17-3. The Spine exercise is the first series of movements performed in the PMCS Drill. It will be the first exercise performed every time in the PMCS Drill even if pain or stiffness appears to originate in another region of the body. Figure 17-1 on page 17-2 illustrates the following movements for the Spine exercise:

- To make sure that the neck is moving properly, compare rotation to the right and left. If there is a loss of motion to one side, this may indicate an issue with a joint in the neck.
- To address the issue, assume the Straddle Stance position before looking up as far as possible without causing pain.
- Repeat this head movement 5 times.
- Perform more repetitions if the exercise improves the issue.
- If there is any pain, seek help from performance readiness experts in the unit.

> ### PMCS CAUTION
> If a Soldier finds an issue in the spine, this must be addressed first before checking the other joints in the body.

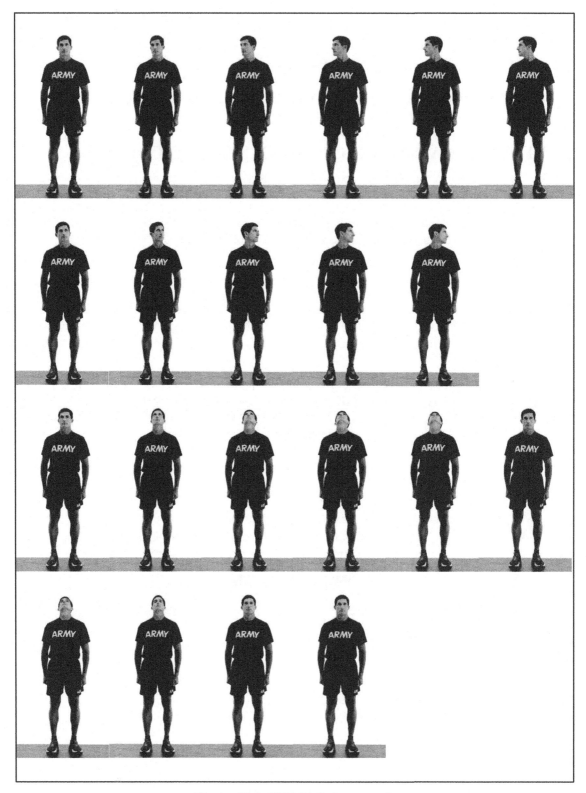

Figure 17-1. PMCS1 Spine—neck

17-4. To make sure that the mid-back is moving properly, the Soldier assumes a seated position with fingers interlocked over the chest before rotating the trunk to the right and left. If there is a loss of motion to one side, this may indicate an issue with a joint in the mid-back (see figure 17-2).

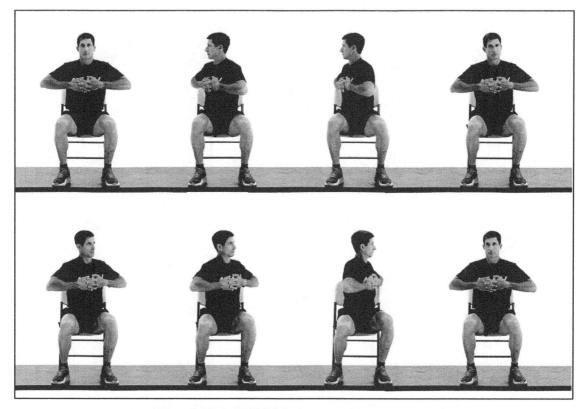

Figure 17-2. PMCS1 Spine—mid-back seated

17-5. See figure 17-3 on page 17-4 for the spine, mid-back standing mobility exercise:

- To address the issue, assume the Straddle Stance position before looking up as far as possible without pain while raising the arms up and over the head.
- Repeat this head movement 5 times.
- Perform more repetitions if the exercise improves the mid-back issue.

Figure 17-3. PMCS1 Spine—mid-back standing mobility

17-6. A modified version may be performed from the Prone position by propping the chin on the tips of the fingers and resting in this position for up to 60 seconds (see figure 17-4). Repeat several times if this improves the mid-back issue. If there is any pain, the Soldier seeks help from performance readiness experts in the unit.

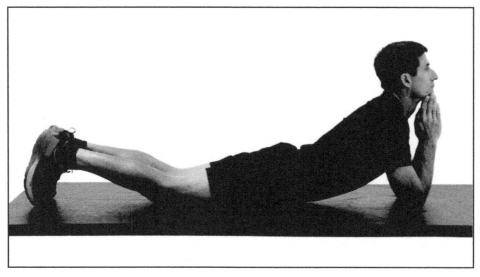

Figure 17-4. PMCS1 Spine—mid-back prone mobility

17-7. To make sure that the low back is moving properly, the Soldier performs the extend movement from the Extend and Flex exercise (see paragraph 16-5). If there is lower back pain or any tightness associated with this movement, this may indicate an issue with a joint in the low back. Figure 17-5 illustrates stretches for the low back. To address the issue, the Soldier repeats the extend movement 10 times moving as far as possible without causing pain.

Figure 17-5. PMCS1 Spine—low back prone

17-8. Another modified version of this exercise, using the same number of repetitions, may be performed from the Straddle Stance position with hands on the low back (see figure 17-6) with the following:
- Perform more repetitions if the exercise improves the issue.
- If there is any pain, seek help from performance readiness experts in the unit.

Figure 17-6. PMCS1 Spine—low back standing

2. ANKLE

17-9. The Ankle exercise mobilizes the joints and muscles around the ankle. Soldiers can use it to check for pain and restricted flexibility and to self-treat for those issues. Soldiers perform the exercise on both ankles to check and compare for pain or stiffness. Figure 17-7 demonstrates the exercise on the left side:

- The starting position for the Ankle exercise is the Half-Kneeling position.
- From the starting position, the Soldier moves the trunk, hips, and knee over the forward foot as far as possible.
- Return to the starting position before repeating the movement 5 times.
- Perform more repetitions if the movement improves the range of motion in the ankle.
- If repeated ankle dorsiflexion does not work, perform kneeling buttock-to-heel movements (see figure 17-8).
- If there is any pain, seek help from performance readiness experts in the unit.

Figure 17-7. PMCS2 Ankle

Figure 17-8. PMCS2 Ankle—kneeling

3. KNEE

17-10.   The Knee exercise mobilizes the joints and muscles around the knee. Soldiers can use it to check for pain and restricted flexibility and to self-treat for those issues. Soldiers perform the exercise on both knees to check and compare for pain or stiffness. Figure 17-9 demonstrates the exercise on the left side:

- The starting position for the Knee exercise is the Straddle Stance position with staggered legs and both hands placed above the knee joint on the front of the thigh.
- From the starting position, contract the quadriceps muscle and press the thigh backwards to further straighten the knee as far as possible.
- Return to the starting position before repeating the movement 5 times.
- Perform more knee extensions if the movement improves the range of motion in the knee.
- If repeated knee extension does not work, perform repeated knee to chest movements from the Supine position (see figure 17-11 on page 17-8).
- If there is any pain, seek help from performance readiness experts in the unit.

Figure 17-9. PMCS3 Knee

4. HIP

17-11.   The Hip exercise mobilizes the joints and muscles around the hip and pelvis. Soldiers can use it to check for pain and restricted flexibility and to self-treat for those issues. Soldiers perform the exercise on both hips to check and compare for pain or stiffness. Figure 17-10 shows the exercise as it would be performed on the left side:

- The starting position for the Hip exercise is the Half-Kneeling position.
- From the starting position, the Soldier moves the trunk, hips, and knee over the forward foot into a deep lunge. The rear knee rests on the ground and the trunk remains upright. This extends the hip of the rear leg and creates a stretch in the front of the rear thigh and pelvis.
- Return to the starting position before repeating the movement 5 times.
- Perform more repetitions if the movement improves the range of motion in the hip.
- If repeated hip extension does not work, perform repeated knee to chest movements from the Supine position (see figure 17-11).
- If there is any pain, seek help from performance readiness experts in the unit.

Figure 17-10. PMCS4 Hip

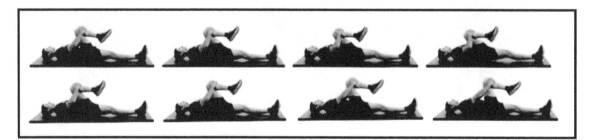

Figure 17-11. PMCS4 Hip—supine

5. SHOULDER

17-12.   The Shoulder exercise mobilizes the joints and muscles around the shoulder girdle. Soldiers can use it to check for pain and restricted flexibility and to self-treat for those issues. Soldiers perform the exercise on both shoulders to check and compare for pain or stiffness. Figure 17-12 illustrates the exercise as it would be performed with a partner to assist (if a partner is not available, the Soldier may use any suitable anchor point such as a wall, suspension trainer, or squat rack):

- The starting position for the Shoulder exercise is the Squat position with arms extended rearward and the hands held by the partner.
- From the starting position, the partner moves the arms up as far as possible to create a 90-degree angle between the arms and the upper back.
- The Soldier squats further until a pain-free end-range is reached.
- Return to the starting position before repeating the movement 5 times.
- Perform more repetitions if the movement improves the range of motion in the shoulder.
- If repeated shoulder extension does not work, try repeated movements into the parade rest position, pulling the wrist with the opposite hand (see figure 17-13).
- If there is any pain, seek help from performance readiness experts in the unit.

Figure 17-12. PMCS5 Shoulder—partner assisted

Figure 17-13. PMCS5 Shoulder

6. ARM

17-13. The Arm exercise mobilizes the joints and muscles around the wrist and elbow. Soldiers can use it to check for pain and restricted flexibility and to self-treat for those issues. Soldiers perform the exercise on both arms to check and compare for pain or stiffness. Figures 17-14 and 17-15 break down the exercise as it would be performed on the left arm:

- The starting position for the Arm exercise is the Straddle Stance position.
- For the elbow—
    - Support the arm with the opposite hand while straightening the elbow as far as possible (see figure 17-14).
    - If the hand can be braced against a wall or other stable object, push the elbow up by the opposite hand to increase the end-range motion.
- For the wrist, keep the elbow straight while using the opposite hand to pull the fingers and hand into extension—the palm will face away from the Soldier (see figure 17-15).
- Return to the starting position before repeating the movement 5 times.
- Perform more repetitions if the movement improves the range of motion in the elbow and wrist.
- If repeated elbow extension does not work, try repeated elbow flexion. The same principle applies to the wrist.
- If there is any pain, seek help from performance readiness experts in the unit.

Figure 17-14. PMCS6 Arm

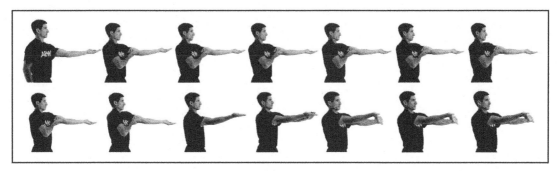

Figure 17-15. PMCS6 Elbow and wrist

This page intentionally left blank.

Source Notes

This division lists sources by chapter.

Chapter 7 Beginning on page 7-1, chapter 7 discusses running methods. Pose Method. Pose Method, Inc. www.PoseMethod.com.

This page intentionally left blank.

Glossary

SECTION I – ACRONYMS AND ABBREVIATIONS

ACFT	Army Combat Fitness Test
ACU	Army combat uniform
ATP	Army techniques publication
CD	conditioning drill (figure caption)
CIMT	United States Army Center for Initial Military Training
CL	climbing drill (figure caption)
ETM	endurance training machine (figure caption)
FM	field manual
FW	free weight training (figure caption)
GD	guerilla drill (figure caption)
H2F	holistic health and fitness
HSD	hip stability drill(figure caption)
LM	landmine drill (figure caption)
MB	medicine ball drill (figure caption)
MMD	military movement drill (figure caption)
P3T	pregnancy and postpartum physical training (figure caption)
PMCS	preventive maintenance checks and services
RUD	running drill (figure caption)
SSD	shoulder stability drill (figure caption)
ST	suspension training drill (figure caption)
STC	strength training circuit (figure caption)
STM	strength training machine (figure caption)
TC	training circular
TRADOC	United States Training and Doctrine Command

Terms included in the glossary are not codified Army terms. They are included for clarity for the reader.

SECTION II – TERMS

aerobic endurance

A component of fitness that involves long-duration, low-intensity physical activity.

agility

The ability to bend, rotate and twist in the frontal, transverse and sagittal planes and use that ability to change direction.

anaerobic endurance

A component of fitness that involves short-duration, high-intensity physical activity.

coordination

The ability to synchronize limb, torso and head movements at varying speeds of motion.

flexibility

The range of motion across single or multiple joints that allows the body to be positioned for optimal movement.

free weight training

Physical training drills consisting of Free Weight Core exercises and Free Weight Assistive exercises.

frontal plane

An imaginary line splitting the body between the front and back.

hand-release push-up

The third event in the Army Combat Fitness Test.

holistic health and fitness

The Army's doctrinal system for physical and nonphysical readiness training of Soldiers.

intensity

The amount of effort exerted to complete an exercise.

leg tuck

The fifth event in the Army Combat Fitness Test.

muscular endurance

A component of fitness that involves sustained bouts of lower intensity strength.

muscular strength

The ability to execute sustained bouts of low intensity movement.

pace

The ability to adjust the speed of an activity to manage fatigue.

perception

The ability to understand correct technique in order to develop skill.

physical readiness

The ability to meet the physical demands of any duty or combat position, move lethally on the battlefield, accomplish the mission and continue to fight, win, and come home healthy.

power

The component of fitness associated with short-duration, explosive movements performed with heavy loads and/or at high speeds.

reconditioning

    Physical training regimens designed to improve or rehabilitate a certain part of the body in order to increase activity or to recover from illness or injury.

recovery

    The period of four to eight weeks when the Soldier begins to prepare for the primary mission. It is characterized by low workloads and general adaptation and recuperation.

running

    A recurring change of support from one foot to the other.

transverse plane

    An imaginary line dividing the body between top and bottom halves.

This page intentionally left blank.

References

All URLs accessed on 31 August 2020.

REQUIRED PUBLICATIONS

These documents must be available to intended users of this publication.

DOD Dictionary of Military and Associated Terms. June 2020. https://www.jcs.mil/Doctrine.

ATP 7-22.01. *Holistic Health and Fitness Testing*. 01 October 2020.

FM 1-02.1 *Operational Terms*. 21 November 2019.

FM 7-22. *Holistic Health and Fitness*. 01 October 2020.

RELATED PUBLICATIONS

These documents are referenced in this publication and contain relevant supplemental information.

Most Army doctrinal publications and Army regulations are available online:
https://armypubs.army.mil/.

FM 6-27/MCTP 11-10C. *The Commander's Handbook on the Law of Land Warfare*. 08 July 2019.

TC 3-21.5. *Drill and Ceremonies*. 20 January 2012.

WEBSITES

Army Combat Fitness Test website. https://www.army.mil/acft/.

Central Army Registry's Holistic Health and Fitness videos.
https://atiam.train.army.mil/catalog/search?current=true&filetype=mp4&respect_date=5%2F1%2F2020&search_terms=CIMT. (Copy and paste this address after accessing the Central Army Registry website if the demonstrations do not populate.)

Medical Readiness Portal.
HTTPS://MEDPROS.MODS.ARMY.MIL/EPROFILE/DEFAULT.ASPX?RETURNURL=%2FEPROFILE%2FADMIN%2FUSERSMANAGER.ASPX.

Pose Method. Pose Method, Inc. www.PoseMethod.com.

PRESCRIBED FORMS

This section contains no entries.

REFERENCED FORMS

Unless otherwise indicated, DA forms are available on the Army Publishing Directorate (APD) Web site at https://armypubs.army.mil/.

DA Form 2028. *Recommended Changes to Publications and Blank Forms.*

DA Form 3349. *Physical Profile*. (Accessible through the Medical Readiness Portal.)

This page intentionally left blank.

Index

Entries are by paragraph number.

180-Degree Landmine, 11-6

180-Degree Landmine Kneeling, 11-11

8-Count Foot Strike, 7-5

8-Count Step-Up, Strength Training Circuit, 13-6

8-Count T Push-Up, 5-23

A

ability, improve running, 7-32
 running challenges, 7-38

activity, drill, 1-23–1-24

agility, improve, 5-18

Alternate ¼-Turn Jump, 5-33

Alternate Pose Pull, 7-22

Alternate Staggered Squat Jump, 5-34

Alternate Twist Jump, 7-15

alternating grip, 2-20

Alternating Grip Pull-Up, Climbing Drill 1, 6-7

Alternating Grip Pull-Up, Climbing Drill 2, 6-13

Alternating Side-Arm Throw, 9-4

Ankle, exercise, 17-9

Arm, exercise, 17-13

assembly, platoon assembly, 1-9

Assisted Lateral Lunge, 10-10

Assisted Single Leg Squat, 10-14–10-15

Assisted Squat, 10-7

B

Back Squat, free weights, 14-6–14-7

Backwards Run, 7-43

balance, improve, 10-9

Battle Buddy, 7-51

Bench Press, 14-10

Bend and Reach, 3-3
 modified, 3-15

Bent-Arm Lateral Raise, 14-20

Bent-Leg Body Twist, 3-12
 modified, 3-23

Bent-Leg Lateral Raise, 4-5

Bent-Over Row, 11-12, 14-16, 13-10

Biceps Curl, 14-24

Decline, 10-8

C

cadence, 1-3

Calf Stretch, 16-9
 modified, 16-19

ceremony, drill and, 1-1–1-8

Change of Support, 7-39

Chest Pass Lateral, 9-3

Chest Press, 15-26–15-28
 modified, 15-27
 Single-Arm, 15-28

Climbing Drill, suspended, 10-16
 types, 6-1

Climbing Drill 1, 6-1–6-7

Climbing Drill 2, exercises, 6-8–6-13

closed grip, 2-14

combat tasks, movement, 4-8, 5-4, 8-6

combinations, Running Drill 6, 7-38–7-43

commands, 1-3
 delivery, 1-5–1-7
 formation assembly, 1-9
 physical training types, 1-4–1-7

Conditioning Drill, types, 5-1–5-34

Conditioning Drill 1, exercises, 5-1–5-7
 modified, 5-8–5-17

Conditioning Drill 2, exercises, 5-18–5-23

Conditioning Drill 3, exercises, 5-24–5-34

confidence, build, 7-23

coordination, improve, 8-1

corrections, Running drill 7, 7-44–7-51

Criss Cross, 7-13

Crossover, 8-8

Crouch Run, 8-9

curl, suspension hamstring, 10-13

D

Deadlift, 14-8–14-9
 single-leg, 5-26
 straight-leg, 11-3, 13-4, 14-9
 sumo, 14-14

Decline Biceps Curl, 10-8

Decline I-T-Y Raise, 10-6

Decline Pull-Up, 10-12

Deep Sumo Squat, 12-8–12-9

Diagonal Chop, 9-5

Diagonal Chop Throw, 9-9

Diagonal Lift to Press, 11-9

Diagonal Press, 11-4

Double-Leg Hop, 7-9

drill, activity, 1-23–1-24
 ceremony and, 1-1–1-8
 guerilla, 6-14–6-17
 physical training, 1-1–1-25
 preparation, 1-17–1-22
 recovery, 1-25
 running, 7-1–7-51
 task and, 1-18

drills, climbing, 6-1–6-13
 conditioning, 5-1–5-34
 landmine, 11-1–11-13
 stability, 4-1–4-13
 suspension training, 10-1–10-16

E

Elevated Pull Back, 7-36

endurance, challenges, 10-1
 improve, 6-1, 6-8
 muscular, 13-1

exercises, advanced, 5-24
 modification, 3-14–3-24
 starting positions, 2-1–2-12

Extend and Flex, 16-5
 modified, 16-14–16-15

F

fall, Running Drill 4, 7-23–7-31

Entries are by paragraph number.

fitness, maintenance, 12-1

Flexed-Arm Hang, Climbing Drill 2, 6-9

Foot Strike, Running Drill 1, 7-1– 7-7

formation, company en masse, 1-13–1-14
company with platoons in column, 1-11–1-12
line, 1-9
platoon extended rectangular formation, 1-15–1-16
positions, 2-1–2-12
reassemble, 1-10–1-16
rectangular, 1-8, 1-15–1-16

Forward Leaning Stance position, 2-6

Forward Lunge, 3-10
modified, 3-21
Strength Training Circuit, 13-5

free weight, types, 14-1, 14-13

Free Weight Assistive, exercises, 14-13–14-26

Free Weight Core Training, exercises, 14-3–14-12

Free Weight Training, core, 14-3–14-12
exercises, 14-1–14-26

Frog Jumps Forward and Backward, 5-32

Front Kick Alternate Toe Touch, 5-28

Front Leaning Rest position, 2-3

Front Squat, free weights, 14-4–14-5

G

Grips, types, 2-13–2-20

Groin Stretch, 16-8
modified, 16-18

Guerilla Drill, exercises, 6-14–6-17

H

Half Jack, 5-21

Half-Kneeling position, 2-11

Half-Squat Laterals, 5-31

Hamstring Stretch, 16-10
modified, 16-20–16-21

Hands Behind, 7-46

Hands in Front, 7-45

Hands on Back, 7-47

Hands on Belly, 7-48

Heel Hook, Climbing Drill 1, 6-4

Climbing Drill 2, 6-10

Heel Raise, 14-15

Heel Run in Place, 7-4

Heel Strike, 7-3

High Jumper, 3-5
modified, 3-17

Hip, exercise, 17-11

Hip Raise Push-Up, 7-16

Hip Stability Drill, exercises, 4-1–4-7

hook grip, 2-19

Hop Forward, 7-41

Hop in Place, 7-40

I

I Raise, 4-9

Incline Bench, 14-11–14-12

Incline Calf Raise, 10-4–10-5

Infantry Run, 7-50

J

jump, alternate ¼-turn, 5-33
alternate staggered squat, 5-34
alternate twist, 7-15
frog, 5-32
modified power, 5-9
power, 5-3
tuck, 5-29

K

Kick Start, 7-37

Knee, exercise, 17-10

Kneeling Side-Arm Throw, 9-10

Kneeling Timber Fall, 7-30

L

L Raise, 4-12

Landmine Drill 1, exercises, 11-1–11-7

Landmine Drill 2, exercises, 11-8–11-13

landmine drills, 11-1–11-13

Lat Pull-Down, 15-14–15-16
single-arm, 15-16
straight-arm, 15-15

lateral, chest pass, 9-3
half-squat, 5-31
Military Movement Drill 1, 8-4

Lateral Leg Raise, 4-3

Lateral Lunge, 11-7

Lateral Raise, 15-9
Bent-Arm, 14-20
Single-Arm, 15-10

leaders, commands, 1-5–1-7
considerations, 1-22

Leg Curl, 15-6–15-8
modified, 15-8

Leg Press, 15-3–15-5
modified, 15-4

Leg Tuck, Climbing Drill 1, 6-6
Climbing Drill 2, 6-12
Strength Training Circuit, 13-13

Leg-Tuck and Pike, suspension, 10-11

Leg-Tuck and Twist, 5-6
modified, 5-14–5-15

Lunge, assisted lateral, 10-10
forward, 3-10, 13-5
forward modified, 3-21
lateral, 11-7
rear, 3-4, 16-4, 11-5
rear modified, 3-16, 16-13
turn and, 5-19

Lunge Walk, 6-16

M

Medial Leg Raise, 4-4

Medicine Ball Drill 1, 9-1–9-7

Medicine Ball Drill 2, 9-8–9-13

Medicine Ball Drills, exercises, 9-1–9-13

Military Movement Drill 1, 8-1–8-5

Military Movement Drill 2, exercises, 8-6–8-9

Military Movement Drills, exercises, 8-1–8-9

mobility, improve, 5-18
increase, 10-9

Modified, Chest Press, 15-27
Conditioning Drill 1, 5-8–5-17
Overhead Press, 15-12
Preparation Drill, 3-14–3-24
Recovery Drill, 16-11–16-20
Sit-Up, 12-5
Triceps Extension, 15-23–15-24
Trunk Extension, 15-21
Trunk Flexion, 15-30

Mountain Climber, 5-5
modified, 5-12–5-13

movement, improve, 6-14, 7-19
increase, 10-9
restore, 17-1

muscle, challenges, 11-1, 11-8
develop, 14-1
endurance building, 13-1

Entries are by paragraph number.

N

neutral grip, 2-18

O

Oblique Sit-Up, 12-4

open grip, 2-15

overhand grip, 2-17

Overhead Arm Pull, 16-3
    modified, 16-12

Overhead Press, 15-11–15-13
    modified, 15-12
    single-arm, 15-13

Overhead Push-Press, 14-19
    Strength Training Circuit,
        13-11

Overhead Triceps Extension,
    14-23

P–Q

Partner Assisted Fall, 7-29

Pelvic Clock, 12-10

Pendulum, 7-14

physical, training drills, 1-1–1-25

physical profile, 3-14

physical training, commands for,
    1-4–1-7
    formation, 1-8

Pony, 7-34

Pose Pull, 7-21
    Alternate, 7-22

Pose Weight Shift, 7-20

positions, formation types, 2-1–
    2-12

Power Jump, 5-3
    modified, 5-9

Power Skip, 8-7

Pregnancy and Postpartum
    Physical Training, exercises,
    12-1–12-10

Preparation Drill, 1-17–1-22
    exercises, 3-1–3-13
    modified, 3-14–3-24
    purpose, 3-1

Preventive Maintenance Checks
    and Services Drills, exercises,
    17-1–17-13

profile, physical, 3-14

Prone position, 2-7

Prone Row, 3-11
    modified, 3-22

pull, Running Drill 5, 7-32–7-37

Pull Back, 7-35

Pull Over, 14-22

pull-up, alternating grip, 6-7, 6-13
    Climbing Drill 1, 6-5
    Climbing Drill 2, 6-11
    decline, 10-12
    Strength Training Circuit, 13-7

Push-Up, 3-13
    8-Count T, 5-23
    hip raise, 7-16
    modified, 3-24
    modified single-leg, 5-16–5-17
    single-leg, 5-7
    single-leg hip raise, 7-17
    Single-Leg Out Hip Raise, 7-18
    suspension, 10-3

R

Rainbow Slam, 9-13

raise, bent-leg lateral, 4-5
    decline I-T-Y, 10-6
    heel, 14-15
    I, 4-9
    incline calf, 10-4–10-5
    L, 4-12
    lateral leg, 4-3
    medial leg, 4-4
    T, 4-10
    W, 4-13
    Y, 4-11

Rear Lunge, 3-4, 11-5, 16-4
    modified, 3-16, 16-13

Rear Lunge to Press, 11-13

Recovery Drill, 1-25, 16-1–16-10
    modified, 16-11–16-20

Recovery Drills, exercises, 16-1–
    16-21
    purpose, 16-1

resistance, advanced, 9-8

Reverse Sit-Up, 12-3

row, bent-over, 11-12, 14-16
    single-arm bent-over, 14-17
    upright, 14-18

Rower, 3-6–3-7
    modified, 3-18

Run in Place 1, 7-6

Run in Place 2, 7-7

Run in Pose, 7-42

Runner's Position, Running Drill 3,
    7-19–7-22

running, improve, 7-44

Running Drill, exercises, 7-1–7-51

Running Drill 1, Foot Strike, 7-1–
    7-7

Running Drill 2, Strength, 7-8–
    7-18

Running Drill 3, Runner's Position,
    7-19–7-22

Running Drill 4, Fall, 7-23–7-31

Running Drill 5, Pull, 7-32–7-37

Running Drill 6, Combinations,
    7-38–7-43

Running Drill 7, Corrections,
    7-44–7-51

S

Seated Row, 15-17–15-19
    single-arm, 15-19
    straight-arm, 15-18

Shin Burn, 7-49

Shoulder, exercise, 17-12

Shoulder Roll, 6-15

Shoulder Stability Drill, exercises,
    4-8–4-13

Shrug, 14-21

Shuttle Sprint, 8-5

Side-to-Side Knee Lifts, 5-27

Single Leg Curl, 15-8

Single Leg Over, 4-7

single Leg Press, 15-5

Single-Arm Bent-Over Row, 14-17

Single-Arm Chest Press, 11-10,
    15-28

Single-Arm Lat Pull-Down, 15-16

Single-Arm Lateral Raise, 15-10

Single-Arm Overhead Press,
    15-13

Single-Arm Seated Row, 15-19

Single-Arm Triceps Extension,
    15-25

Single-Leg Curl, modified, 15-7

Single-Leg Deadlift, 5-26

Single-Leg Hip Raise Push-Up,
    7-17

Single-Leg Hop, 7-10

Single-Leg Out Hip Raise
    Push-Up, 7-18

Single-Leg Over, 16-7
    modified, 16-17

Single-Leg Press, 15-5

Single-Leg Push-Up, 5-7
    modified, 5-16–5-17

Single-Leg Tuck, 4-6

Sitting position, 2-12

Sit-Up, modified, 12-5
    oblique, 12-4
    reverse, 12-3

Sit-Up Throw, 9-12

Six-Point Stance position, 2-4

Entries are by paragraph number.

Skip in Place, 7-11

Slam, 9-6

Soldier Carry, 6-17

Spine, exercise, 17-3–17-8

spotter, Back Squat, 14-7
    Bench Press, 14-12
    Front Squat, 14-5
    Incline Bench, 14-12

Sprint Start, 7-31

Squat, assisted, 10-7
    assisted single leg, 10-14–
      10-15
    back, 14-6–14-7
    deep sumo, 12-8–12-9
    free weights, 14-4–14-7
    front, 14-4–14-5
    position, 2-2
    sumo, 13-3
    Y, 5-25

Squat Bender, 3-8
    modified, 3-19

stability drills, 4-1–4-13
    hip, 4-1–4-7
    shoulder, 4-8–4-13

Standing Trunk Curve, 12-6–12-7

Straddle Run Forward and
    Backward, 5-30

Straddle Stance position, 2-5

Straight-Arm Lat Pull-Down, 15-15

Straight-Arm Pull, Climbing Drill 1,
    6-3
    Strength Training Circuit, 13-8

Straight-Arm Seated Row, 15-18

Straight-Leg Deadlift, 11-3, 14-9
    Strength Training Circuit, 13-4

strength, build, 9-1
    challenges, 11-1, 11-8
    develop, 14-1
    improve, 5-18, 7-8
    Running Drill 2, 7-8–7-18

upper body, 6-1

Strength Training Circuit,
    exercises, 13-1–13-13

Strength Training Machine Drill,
    exercises, 15-1–15-30

Strength Training Machines, 15-1

Stretch Cord Fall, 7-28

Sumo Deadlift, 14-14

Sumo Squat, Strength Training
    Circuit, 13-3

Sumo Wall Throw, 9-11

Supine Bicycle, 5-20

Supine Body Twist, Strength
    Training Circuit, 13-12

Supine Chest Press, Strength
    Training Circuit, 13-9

Supine position, 2-8–2-10

Suspended Climbing Drills, 10-16

Suspension Hamstring Curl, 10-13

Suspension Leg-Tuck and Pike,
    10-11

Suspension Push-Up, 10-3

Suspension Training Drills, 10-1–
    10-16

Sustaining Phase, Climbing Drill
    2, 6-8

Swimmer, 5-22

T

T Raise, 4-10

task, drill and, 1-18

Thigh Stretch, 16-6
    modified, 16-16

throw, alternating side-arm, 9-4
    kneeling side-arm, 9-10
    sit-up, 9-12
    sumo wall, 9-11
    underhand wall, 9-7

Timber Fall, 7-24

Timber Fall in Pose, 7-25

Toes In and Out, 7-12

Triceps Extension, 15-21–15-25
    modified, 15-23–15-24
    Single-Arm, 15-25

Trunk Extension, 15-20
    modified, 15-21

Trunk Flexion, 15-29
    modified, 15-30

Tuck Jump, 5-29

Turn and Lunge, 5-19

Twist Jump, Alternate, 7-15

U

underhand grip, 2-16

Underhand Wall Throw, 9-7

Upright Row, 14-18

V

Vertical, 8-3

V-Up, 5-4
    modified, 5-10–5-11

W–X

W Raise, 4-13

Walk Progression, 7-33

Wall Fall, 7-26

Wall Fall in Pose, 7-27

warm up, 1-22

Weighted Trunk Extension, 14-26

Weighted Trunk Flexion, 14-25

Windmill, 3-9
    modified, 3-20

Y–Z

Y Raise, 4-11

Y Squat, 5-25

By Order of the Secretary of the Army:

JAMES C. MCCONVILLE
General, United States Army
Chief of Staff

Official:

KATHLEEN S. MILLER
Administrative Assistant
to the Secretary of the Army
2026202

DISTRIBUTION:
Active Army, Army National Guard, and United States Army Reserve: To be distributed in accordance with the initial distrubution number (IDN) 116106, requirements for ATP 7-22.02.

Army ACFT FY20 Standards (As of 1 Oct 19)

Points	MDL	SPT	HRP	SDC	LTK	2MR	
100	340	12.5	60	1:33	20	13:30	
99		12.4	59	1:36		13:39	
98		12.2	58	1:39	19	13:48	
97	330	12.1	57	1:41		13:57	
96		11.9	56	1:43	18	14:06	
95		11.8	55	1:45		14:15	
94	320	11.6	54	1:46	17	14:24	
93		11.5	53	1:47		14:33	
92	310	11.3	52	1:48	16	14:42	
91		11.2	51	1:49		14:51	
90	300	11.0	50	1:50	15	15:00	
89		10.9	49	1:51		15:09	
88	290	10.7	48	1:52	14	15:18	
87		10.6	47	1:53		15:27	
86	280	10.4	46	1:54	13	15:36	
85		10.3	45	1:55		15:45	
84	270	10.1	44	1:56	12	15:54	
83		10.0	43	1:57		16:03	
82	260	9.8	42	1:58	11	16:12	
81		9.7	41	1:59		16:21	
80	250	9.5	40	2:00	10	16:30	
79		9.4	39	2:01		16:39	
78	240	9.2	38	2:02	9	16:48	
77		9.1	37	2:03		16:57	
76	230	8.9	36	2:04	8	17:06	
75		8.8	35	2:05		17:15	
74	220	8.6	34	2:06	7	17:24	
73		8.5	33	2:07		17:33	
72	210	8.3	32	2:08	6	17:42	
71		8.2	31	2:09		17:51	
70	200	8.0	30	2:10	5	18:00	HVY
69		7.8	28	2:14		18:12	
68	190	7.5	26	2:18	4	18:24	
67		7.1	24	2:22		18:36	
66		6.8	22	2:26		18:48	
65	180	6.5	20	2:30	3	19:00	SIG
64	170	6.2	18	2:35		19:24	
63	160	5.8	16	2:40		19:48	
62	150	5.4	14	2:45	2	20:12	
61		4.9	12	2:50		20:36	
60	140	4.5	10	3:00	1	21:00	MOD
59				3:01		21:01	
58				3:02		21:03	
57				3:03		21:05	
56				3:04		21:07	
55		4.4	9	3:05		21:09	
54				3:06		21:10	
53				3:07		21:12	
52				3:08		21:14	
51				3:09		21:16	
50	130	4.3	8	3:10		21:18	

Army ACFT FY20 Standards (As of 1 Oct 19)

Points	MDL	SPT	HRP	SDC	LTK	2MR
49						21:19
48				3:11		21:21
47						21:23
46				3:12		21:25
45		4.2	7			21:27
44				3:13		21:28
43						21:30
42				3:14		21:32
41						21:34
40	120	4.1	6	3:15		21:36
39						21:37
38				3:16		21:39
37						21:41
36				3:17		21:43
35		4.0	5			21:45
34				3:18		21:46
33						21:48
32				3:19		21:50
31						21:52
30	110	3.9	4	3:20		21:54
29						21:55
28				3:21		21:57
27						21:59
26				3:22		22:01
25		3.8	3			22:03
24				3:23		22:04
23						22:06
22				3:24		22:08
21						22:10
20	100	3.7	2	3:25		22:12
19						22:13
18				3:26		22:15
17						22:17
16				3:27		22:19
15		3.6	1			22:21
14				3:28		22:22
13						22:24
12				3:29		22:26
11						22:28
10	90	3.5		3:30		22:30
9						22:31
8				3:31		22:33
7						22:35
6				3:32		22:37
5		3.4				22:39
4				3:33		22:40
3						22:42
2				3:34		22:44
1						22:46
0	80	3.3	0	3:35	0	22:48

ACFT 2.0: Changes sparked by COVID-19

FORT EUSTIS, Va. – The Army Combat Fitness Test, or ACFT, will be the force's test of record Oct. 1, but the Army's top enlisted Soldier says troops will have more time to train for and pass the six-event test -- without fear of it negatively impacting their careers during that time.
Despite hold ups caused by COVID-19, Sgt. Maj. of the Army Michael A. Grinston is confident the long-planned ACFT will stay on track. In addition to the new training timeline, he also announced a handful of other modifications to the test, dubbing it ACFT 2.0.

It's the same six-event physical fitness test -- just an updated version, Grinston said. So even though troops don't have to pass the test this year, they still have to take the ACFT as scheduled.
"When it's the test of record, you have to put it into the system of record, and that's the only requirement right now," Grinston said. This means the Army won't take administrative actions against Soldiers for potential ACFT failures.

Potential career impacts like separation, derogatory or referred evaluation reports, and a Soldier's Order of Merit List standing are all off the table to be negatively impacted due to an ACFT failure. This news comes as the Army, in response to social distancing guidelines, hit the brakes on all physical fitness tests in March. Although fitness tests slowed down, Army leaders went full-steam ahead to plan how Soldiers will jump from the 40-year-old Army Physical Fitness Test, or APFT, to the new ACFT 2.0.

So what are the changes?

First, for many, the APFT is gone for good. Once testing suspensions are lifted, the only Soldiers required to take an APFT ever again will be troops without a current passing score, the sergeant major confirmed.

"As for everyone else [with a current passing APFT score] -- they should start training for the ACFT," he added.

As far as the evolution of the ACFT, the biggest change for Soldiers is the option to substitute a two-minute plank, once a Soldier has attempted the leg tuck.

The other six events are still locked in; the 3 repetition maximum dead-lift, standing power throw, hand release pushups, leg tuck, 2-mile run, and sprint, drag, carry. The plank is just an interim assessment.

The plank is seen as a transitioning tool for Soldiers jumping from the APFT to the six ACFT events, said Maj. Gen. Lonnie G. Hibbard, the U.S. Army Center for Initial Military Training commanding general.

Depending on an individual's physical starting point, switching back to the leg tuck should take "anywhere between six to three months," Hibbard added, but for now, the plank is an alternative. Planks are a core muscle-burning exercise, completed by individuals who remain static with their elbows planted to the ground directly beneath the shoulders at a 90-degree angle while maintaining a straight posture.

Plank exercises can be conducted almost anywhere, Hibbard said, and do not require equipment to train for. Under the current COVID-19 conditions, this could be an ideal transitional assessment. Also, the stationary bike event dropped its initial 15,000-meter standard down to a 12,000-meter standard. Biking is an Alternate Assessment for Soldiers with permanent profiles unable to complete the two-mile run.

Additional changes for fiscal year 2021 also include scoring standards. All Soldiers are challenged to pass the ACFT at the "Gold Standard," Hibbard confirmed, which is an overall minimum total score of 60.

To pass, all troops are required to meet the moderately challenging "gold standard" instead of the more grueling "grey or black" scoring minimums -- typically reserved for harsher, more physically demanding career fields. This standard applies to all Soldiers, regardless of age or gender.
Until COVID-19 hit, "we were seeing vast improvements with the ACFT," Grinston said, adding the changes to the ACFT promotes a better physical fitness standard that will mirror the physical demands of the Army, while also decreasing injuries and having more effective Soldiers within the ranks.

Made in the USA
Coppell, TX
02 March 2022

74345365R00149